PUB WALKS
in the
PENNINES

Les Lumsdon and Colin Speakman

SIGMA LEISURE, Wilmslow, England

First published in 1991 by Sigma Leisure - an imprint of Sigma Press, 1 South Oak Lane, Wilmslow, Cheshire SK9 6AR, England.

Whilst every effort has been made to ensure that the information given in this book is correct, neither the publisher nor the author accept any responsibility for any inaccuracy.

British Library Cataloguing in Publication Data
A CIP record for this book is available from the British Library.

ISBN: 1-85058-261-0

Maps by
Pam Upchurch

Typesetting and design by
Sigma Hi-Tech Services Ltd, Wilmslow

Printed and bound by
Manchester Free Press, Paragon Mill, Jersey St., Manchester M4 6FP.

PREFACE

Pubs and walking have always gone together, ever since medieval pilgrims made their way to a village inn or country tavern to enjoy a local brew and swap travellers' tales. When people had to walk miles to visit their places of workship, thoughtful priests ensured an inn was opened close by the church so that, after the Credos and the Sanctus, a pot (or two) of frothy ale could be enjoyed before making the way home.

The modern rambler, armed with a Pathfinder map, is still able to trace those medieval parishioners' ways across former open fields or fellsides, used by our forefathers for more centuries than anyone can guess. Several of such routes are to be found in the pages of this book.

The Pennines are particularily rich in old tracks and pathways which, because of the region's topography, have defied both time and the destructive curse of tarmac, making superb routes for the modern rambler. There are also some exceptionally good pubs to be found on such routes, many supplying ales produced with the help of fast-flowing Pennine springs.

We have collected thirty such walks, many of them circular, some of them point to point but all are equally easily accessible for car drivers and public transport users. However, we confess a strong bias towards public transport usage, because drivers should not drink and drive and where cheap, easily accessible public transport exists (as it does with every one of these walks), it makes good environmental sense to use it. Otherwise the driver of the party should be prepared to stay on soft drinks or low alcohol brews, which, with so much real ale around, seems a little unfair.

The authors practice what they preach: each of these walks was therefore planned and researched using public transport which is generally easily and readily available on any day of the week, including, in most instances, Sundays, and details of which are supplied with each walk.

Each is a carefully planned country walk, sometimes with an urban element, varying in length from between four and eight miles, and with a prospect of an excellent pint at the beginning, middle or end of none-too-strenuous exertions.

We would not pretend for a moment that our collection is even remotely exhaustive. So many fine Pennine pubs and walks have had to be left out for reasons of space that there is material enough for a future volume. Let this merely be an introduction to just some of the pubs and walks to and from them in the Pennines which are available to the discerning walker.

Our gratitude is extended to that great campaigning body CAMRA (Campaign for Real Ale) which has done so much to raise awareness and standards among both producers and consumers of local ale. Thanks also go to the publicans who have welcomed us and served us with excellent pints of ale, and very often good food.

We look forward to sharing with you the pleasures of meandering Pennine footpaths and some equally memorable pints.

Les Lumsdon and Colin Speakman

CONTENTS

THE PENNINES

The Backbone of England

The Pennines is a long, meandering range of hills some two hundred miles long and between twenty and thirty miles wide. It stretches from the English Midlands to the Scottish border, bisecting the North of England, dividing Cheshire from Derbyshire, Lancashire from Yorkshire, Cumbria from Durham and Northumberland, along one of the most significant watersheds of the British Isles.

These hills have been around for at least 300 million years, when the predominantly Carboniferous sedimentary rocks from which they were formed were laid down as the beds of ancient seas carrying the skeletons of millions of living creatures that fossilised to limestone. Vast sandy-sea estuaries compressed to coarse sandstones and millstone grit, primeval forests fossilised to coal. Elevation by vast subterranean pressures to truly Alpine height during the Tertiary period some 65 million years ago was followed by millenia of erosion by the elements. The subsequent action of great glaciers produced the characteristic flat-topped Pennine landforms and deep valleys so familiar to the modern traveller.

The Human Impact

Human settlement, initially on the drier slopes and less thickly wooded terraces above the dense swamp and forest of the valleys, began an ever accelerating process of change. Gradually, the first hunters were replaced by waves of more sophisticated farmers whose clearances made space for the first permanent settlements. The tool makers of Iron and Bronze Age eventually yielded to Celtic warriors and farmers whose civilisation still has a faint echo in many of the place names – especially river names – of the present day. They, in turn, were largely, but not entirely, replaced by successive invading generations of Germanic tribes, Angles,

Saxon, and eventually Danes and Vikings. These are the ancestors of the modern inhabitants of the Pennines who cleared the forests and whose settlements, including farmsteads, occupy sites that have been in constant use for a thousand years or more.

Yet even from earliest times, the Pennines have been a severe barrier to humankind, the thin upland soils and elevated position exposed to ferocious winds, rain and blizzards from the Irish Sea or Plain of York. Travel across the hills from east to west until relatively recently, remained difficult and was confined to a handful of deep passes linked by exposed moorland tracks, all quickly closed by winter blizzards. Even in the age of the motorway and Inter-City express, North-south travel along the Pennines remains problematic with few roads and only one major railway – the celebrated Settle-Carlisle line – sharing a north south configuration along the rooftop of England.

'Pennines' – a recent invention

The name Pennines for this long chain of hills is relatively young, and owes nothing to its earlier inhabitants. It was not used until the 18th century when one Charles Betram, a young Professor of English in Copenhagen University, produced what turned out to be a forged medieval monastic manuscript which supposedly described Britain as being divided by the 'Pennine Alps'. However, some two centuries earlier the Elizabethan traveller Camden in 1586 in his Latin description of his journeys through Britain in 'Britannia' had compared the range of hills as being 'like the Apennine in Italy', a name which was to have an echo in later years.

The term was taken up by the geologists William Conybeare and John Philips writing in 1822. In later years an extra 'e' was added as the term came into general use to describe the 'chain' of hills which lay between Staffordshire and Scotland.

The Pennine Way was only completed in 1965, as Britain's first long distance trail. This 250 mile walking route between Edale in the Derbyshire Peaks and Kirk Yetholm on the Scottish Border has given the name 'Pennine' a new significance and romance for walkers.

It is now generally assumed that 'Pennines' includes:

❑ the northern part of the Peak District, particular the 'Dark' Peak, around Longdendale;

❑ the areas of the Colne, Holme, Tame and Calder and Aire Valleys of the old West Riding in what is now known as the South Pennines;

❑ the Central Pennines, more usually known as the Yorkshire Dales; and

❑ the North Pennines, which is the area between the Stainmore Pass (the A66) and the Scottish Border.

This book concentrates on the larger centres of population in the southern part of the Pennines. The areas chosen include the western and northern edges of the Peak district, the South Pennines, parts of the Yorkshire Dales and, as a special tribute to the Settle-Carlisle railway, just one favourite walk from Appleby Station to the very edge of the North Pennines.

A Unique Region

So what is it that makes the Pennines special?

They are not high hills by European standards, the highest peak, Cross Fell in the North Pennines, being less than 3,000 feet or 900 metres above sea level. Most Pennine summits lie between 1,500 and 2,400 feet (450-600 metres), being little more than long, exposed ridges of high moorland.

What they lack in height they make up for in grandeur and, to be truthful, inhospitality. The smooth, rounded summits which form the horizon above many a Pennine mill village or market town, rise in scale out of the narrow valleys. They make it impossible to look up and not see wild places, nor be impressed by the power and beauty of the natural world.

Summits

The summits themselves are bleak places, often with little more than thin, windswept moorgrass or rough pasture. There are acres of heather, richly purple in late summer, and dark, acid cottongrass which in late spring breaks to feathery tufts of white bog cotton. Often there is only dark peat bog, deep and treacherous sphagnum bog or a lunar landscape of peat craters, dark and uninviting. But sometimes wind-carved outcrops of gritstone form distinctive crags that make useful landmarks and offer superb viewpoints across the surrounding valleys.

The moors are havens for wildlife, particularly bird life such as the diminutive skylark whose tiny hovering form and shrill music is the delight of any Spring morning. Listen to the evocative curlew and lapwing and watch the spectacular birds of prey that hover for hours seeking thermals above the moor edges – kestrels, sparrowhawks, even the occasional buzzard.

Drystone walls and Common Land

Countless thousands of miles of drystone wall criss-cross these Pennine moors and summits, dividing the fell and moortops into great sheep walks, carving up the hillside pastures and lower slopes into countless smaller fields.

These drystone walls are recent in origin, dating from the 18th and early 19th centuries when, after various Enclosure Acts, the old common fields of the upland parishes were allotted to various landowners, the dispossessed commoners working for small wages to build the enclosure walls. Because so much of the Pennines remained as wild, uncultivable land, more great areas of common grazing land remained unenclosed compared with many other parts of Britain. These areas of common which happened to be in former Urban District Council territory (much of the South Pennines) enjoy, thanks to a small clause in the 1925 Law of Property Act, full legal right of public access, a right long denied rural commons thanks to an unholy alliance of landowners and grouseshooters with influence that makes a mockery of modern democratic processes.

Many of the moorland areas have, for the last century or so, been water gathering grounds for the huge industrial areas which lie so very close to the Pennines and in some cases on their foothills. Vast reservoirs sometimes entirely fill little side valleys and are a dominant feature of the upland landscape. The catchwater drains to them sometimes provide useful walking routes in otherwise empty moorland.

Secret Valleys

But there are unspoiled, still secret side valleys down which streams cascade, and the natural woodlands – birch, oak, ash, alder, holly – that have long since vanished from the eroded uplands still survive, perhaps carpeted with bluebells and even primroses in Spring. Such places, with their waterfalls and delicate beauty, are particularly precious and need to be protected, their very beauty enhanced by the bleakness of the surrounding moorlands. They too, are rich in wildlife, an abundance of woodland birds, small mammals and insects.

Farming Patterns

Farming in the Pennines has always been difficult, with earlier attempts at arable farming – mainly oats – soon yielding to hillgrazing, cattle and, predominantly, sheep, the tougher breeds such as Swaledales and Dalesbreds, capable of withstanding the harsh winter conditions.

On the high moorland stone-built farms are still to be found which often date back to Tudor or Jacobean times, with ornate datestones over their front doors and narrow top storey weavers' windows which reflect a time when handloom weaving was essential to supplement the subsistence farming of the high moors.

There are still, in the South Pennines in particular, small former weaving settlements, hamlets or even entire villages such as Heptonstall (see Walk 19) which have changed little in outward appearance since the seventeenth century, give or take the odd television aerial and the Toyota parked outside what used to be a barn. Much as the purist may regret the gentrification and urbanisation of these communities as a result of the motorcar, the alternative would be dereliction and demolition of whole settlements as the reason for their existence vanished into history.

The Pennine Valleys

Between the high moors lie valleys which in the South Pennines are, or were, largely industrial. The power of countless moorland streams has been harnessed to drive waterwheels, and later to provide the water for steam power of countless cotton or worsted mills. The more isolated water-powered mills of the late eighteenth and early nineteenth centuries yielded to the larger coal powered mills along the canal sides or close to the railways with their cheap supplies of bulk coal and raw material.

Around such mills grew up the typical mill towns of the Pennines. Close by the mill stood the grand millowners' mansions, neo-classically proportioned to the designs of architects; nearby the larger terraces of the mill manager, and then the long, usually parallel rows of millworkers' dwellings, usually built in sturdy stone and, sometimes, as in Calderdale, clinging perilously, storey above storey, to the steep hillside.

We confess a particularly fascination for this kind of mill-and-moors scenery of the Pennines. The streets themselves are often linked by narrow alleyways or "ginnells", usually cobbled or with steps worn smooth by generations of clog-shod feet, often enclosed between gritstone walls green with lichen. Such ways provided the most direct paths between villages, and again to pub, school and church, before motorised transport, and are still important for local people and for ramblers.

The Human Scale

A sense of place in the Pennines is all these things, together with the gaunt mill chimneys, canal banks, railway lines and roads. These sometimes crowd into the valley bottom, often overlooked by a breathtakingly beautiful curve of fellside, with hanging woods, forming a majestic backcloth to a landscape which in spite of the depredations of urban sprawl, retains its special qualities. Perhaps this is because it is on a human scale compared with the brutal wastelands of featureless suburbia the twentieth century has created around every town and city. The endless dreary expanses of supermarkets and cash and carry warehouses intersected by high-speed urban freeways are what the car culture will bequeath to the next generations.

Yorkshire Dales

This is equally true of the higher Yorkshire Dales, in the limestone areas. Modern motor tourists see little of the old traces of industry which are still to be discerned on the hillsides – remains of old textile mills, lead mines, old mine entrances or levels, spoil tips, mill races, telling of a time when people living in Dales villages had to earn their living in other ways. Retirement cottages and comfortable second homes in many a Dales village once housed large families eeking a living from subsistence farming, weaving or leadmining, and sometimes form a combination of all three. Tourism may not be a panacea but it at least provides some jobs and help to small businesses in the Pennines. Computer technology is encouraging new rural industries in areas which would otherwise have become retreats for the elderly and the affluent.

Perhaps that is another reason why we have focussed more attention on the busier, South Pennines which in many ways are still much more of a working landscape, rather than just a tourist region. Where in spite of recession and overseas competition, there are still working mills manufacturing real cloth, where engineering still takes place and people come home from work wearing overalls and have dirty hands.

Not everyone in this part of the Pennines has two cars. A substantial majority of the population of areas like Calderdale, the Colne Valley and areas like Keighley do not have one, but there are still plenty of buses and quite a few trains to get them about, which make them very civilised places for the non-driving walker.

Pennine people

The character of the Pennines is in the people as much as the landscape.

It's an area where life has always been hard, winters long and summers short (Defoe's famous description of snow on Blackstone Edge in August will surprise few Pennine Wayfarers). Whether it was pre-industrial revolution farming or in the Industrial Revolution itself, which began in these Pennine valleys, survival has always been a battle against the elements.

So the Pennines have created a people noted for their stoicism and resilience, who over the centuries have seen more bad times than good and who are, of necessity, great survivors. To such people the thought of bank interest rates and mortgages are of little more account than the unexpectedly harsh wind that prematurely whitens the felltops in November. They also have a great sense of humour, a laconic wit that takes times to get used to. To let your face 'crack' as they say on the Yorkshire side of the Pennines, is to give the joke away.

The human culture of the Pennines has created a complexity and diversity within the countryside and townscape which is there to be discovered and experienced. There is no better way to begin to understand what the Pennines are all about than as a rambler, on your own two feet close to the sounds, sights, scents and feel of this very special areas of England. Add to that the sense of taste and you have another irrefutable reason on your ramble for calling at a Pennine pub.

Some Practical Points

Even if you plan only a short walk in the Pennines, it pays to have strong footwear, preferable at least lightweight boots, and, inevitably, rainwear and an extra sweater. Always carry some emergency food supplies with you.

The sketch maps in the book are for guidance only, and we urge that you take the relevant map – preferably the Ordnance Survey 1:25,000 Pathfinder or Outdoor Leisure sheet listed for each walk, or at very least the relevant 1:50,000 Landranger map which because it covers a greater area, works out less expensive, but doesn't show such important details as field boundaries.

All the suggested routes in this book are either on public rights of way or well established permissive routes, and all were free of obstruction at the time of survey. If there are problems, please note them preferably with a grid reference and write to: the County Surveyor in a Shire County; to the Chief Technical Services Officer of the relevant Metropolitan Borough in a former Metropolitan County (i.e. Greater Manchester or West Yorkshire); or to the National Park Officer in the

Peak or Yorkshire Dales National Park. Alternatively, local branches of the Ramblers' Association may be able to help.

Public transport information is contained either in the British Rail national timetable or local train guides (available at any manned station) or, bus and rail, from the following public transport enquiry lines (in most cases during office hours only):

Cheshire: 0244 602666

Derbyshire: 0322 292200

Lancashire: 0772 263333

Greater Manchester: 061 228 7811

South Yorkshire: 0742 768688

West Yorkshire: 0532 457676

Where (at time of writing) bargain unlimited travel tickets exist, including the West Yorkshire Metro Day Rover (an off-peak ticket covering all rail and bus services in West Yorkshire), the Wayfarer ticket (similar for the whole of Greater Manchester and the Peak District of Derbyshire) and the NorthWest Ranger (a day ticket on Network Northwest services) these are listed in the text. For costs and availability enquire locally.

Two organisations that all readers of this book should belong to are the Ramblers Association (details of membership: 1/5 Wandsworth Road, London, SW8 2XX) and CAMRA (details of membership: 34 Alma Road, St. Albans, Herts, AL1 3BW).

Colin Speakman – one of the authors – at the Kings Arms, Heath (Walk 15)

PENNINE PUBS

What makes a good pub?

It is too easy to say 'the beer' though good, well kept real ale is a pre-requisite for any self-respecting pub. A good pub must have other qualities besides.

Mock-Tudor Creations

Perhaps it is easier to suggest what doesn't make a good pub. Featureless, modern road-houses, surrounded by huge car parks, with shopping precinct architecture or hideous concrete facades are rarely good pubs. Neither are artificial mock-Tudor creations, with rusticated beams, quilted plastic seats, pseudo-antique horse brasses, or various kinds or ersatz memorabilia rather than anything which is real or belongs to the place it is. We confess a prejudice against juke boxes, especially over-loud ones, and piped music whether pop, rock or Rachmaninov.

Sometimes a lovely old Georgian or even Jacobean facade conceals an interior which has been gutted and recreated with some brewers' standardised old world pub kit. At the other extreme, no one enjoys a dirty, grotty, run-down drinking den, which hasn't seen a lick of paint in years with grubby seats and stub-end scorched tables.

Often it is a different kind of failing. The exterior may be authentic, the interior if not period at least a tasteful recreation, and real ale readily available, but the whole place may have been turned over to 'yuppiedom' in ways that suggest quite clearly that walkers who wear outdoor clothing and might even have mucky boots are not at all welcome compared with the well coiffured motorists and sophisticated lounge lizards that form the usual clientele.

Having said that, if you have been battling with the elements, including muddy fields, it is only courtesy to use the tap room rather than the lounge, and if necessary leave muddy boots in the entrance porch together with over large rucksacks – though a small day sack should be adequate for all these walks.

So what makes a really good pub?

Gemütlichkeit

The Germans, who know a thing or two about good pubs and real beer, have a word for a pub or eatery which is quite untranslatable – *Gemütlichkeit*. This means comfort, friendliness, a welcoming atmosphere, a feeling of belonging. Such pubs will have their regulars, but strangers will not be made to feel unwelcome amongst them, providing of course they don't dominate the place.

Part of the pleasure of good pubs is real people, local folk who have time to chat to a stranger, know a little bit about the village or town in which they live, but are happy to keep themselves to themselves.

The decor might be plain, even ordinary, but if a place has the right feel to it, it has Gemütlichkeit.

Of course, these things are personal, and one person's ideal pub is another person's horror story. So be it. Authors' privilege is to know and describe what we like. All our pubs have welcomed us as ordinary walkers, buying a pint or a pint and a sandwich. All sell 'real', cask-conditioned, ale, and most sell food.

Food

Food in pubs is one of the success stories of the last decade. Pub food now represents the best value for money in British catering with often excellent hot meals available for well under a fiver. For many pubs, the sale of food is an important part of otherwise vulnerable profit margins, and for that reason most publicans will hardly take kindly to people eating their own food in their bars. Having paid your train or bus fare (or even petrol) for the day, and the price of a pint, why not enjoy a bite with your pint? A hot snack can add to enjoyment. Not all pubs in this

v

book serve food all days of the week, and if you are planning to have lunch at a particular pub on a particular day it might be worthwhile checking in advance.

The Haychatter, Bradfield Dale (Walk 4)

Real Ale

Good ale is to be found throughout the Pennines. We hardly need retell here the story of the Campaign for Real Ale (CAMRA) which, during the 1970s, successfully managed to reverse the trend to bright, gassy, "keg" beers. Through a remarkable consumer revolution they brought about the revival in fortunes of the hand-pulled beer engine (many of them made, incidentally in the Pennines), and excellent ale to go in them. Ale is the older English name for a brew made from fermented malt, which was only overtaken by a fashion for Dutch 'beer' (a foretaste of the lager phenomenon) to which hops were added for flavour in the seventeenth century; since that time the names "ale" and "beer" have become virtually interchangeable.

Through CAMRA's activities, not only have many small breweries enjoyed a modest revival of fortune, with many locally produced beers on the brink of extinction enjoying a welcome revival. New local beers, sometimes produced in small, local breweries have appeared on the market, recalling a golden era when beers were always brewed locally and delivered only as far as a horse and dray could travel. This is a world of difference from travelling in high speed antiseptic tanks up and down the motorway network at colossal waste of energy and addition to the greenhouse effect.

But even the keg beers have been upstaged in their turn by even more insipid lagers, many of them bearing bogus German names or even genuine German names used on totally un-German products. Thanks to massive advertising campaigns, lager with its higher profit margin, now outsells beer in the UK, especially among the young.

Worried by the impact of the real ale revolution at the other end of the market, with the success of such small independents as Theakston's and

The Fleece, Addingham (Walk 25)

Thwaites, the large brewery conglomerates and leisure corporations who had originally sneered at what they described as real ale fanatics, fought back. In some cases long neglected ales of their own were brought back onto the market. To be fair to at least one of the largest companies, Leeds-based Tetley's never entirely abandoned hand-pulled real ales from many of their smaller pubs and soon re-introduced it elsewhere when the climate of opinion began to change. In other cases good new real beers were brought onto the market.

More dubiously, names of once highly regarded independent breweries such as Castle Eden were brought to the fore or, like Boddington's of Manchester or Theakston's of Masham, were bought out, and whilst the beers are still good, they no longer have the local character they once had.

Champion

CAMRA, quite properly, continues to champion the cause of the small independent breweries, which are an integral part of the culture and taste of the area in which they are produced. Why shouldn't small independent producers thrive alongside the giants? In the Black Forest of Germany, an area about the same size as the Pennines, it is possible to find over 1,000 different varieties of beer on offer. Both the nationally and regionally known brands and names, but much more interesting, the products of superb little village breweries. It will be a sad day for British beer if you can no longer taste Clark's in Wakefield, Thwaite's around Lancashire, Timothy Taylor's in Airedale and Calderdale, Dent Bitter in Dent.

It is perhaps worth repeating the warning: drinking and driving don't mix. If you are the driver of your party, please keep off the ale. Best of all, help reduce congestion and pollution and make the trip by bus and train. It can be part of the fun.

The information supplied in this book was correct when going to press, but changes occur all the time. Tenancies, landlords and landladies move, circumstances differ, breweries change, 'modernisation' (not always welcome) occurs and neither authors nor publishers can accept responsibility for any problems caused by changing conditions.

Key to Sketch Maps

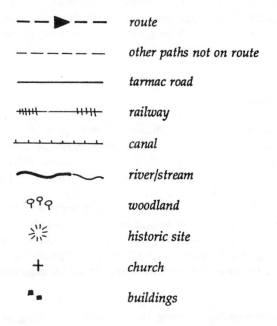

route

other paths not on route

tarmac road

railway

canal

river/stream

woodland

historic site

church

buildings

General Location Map

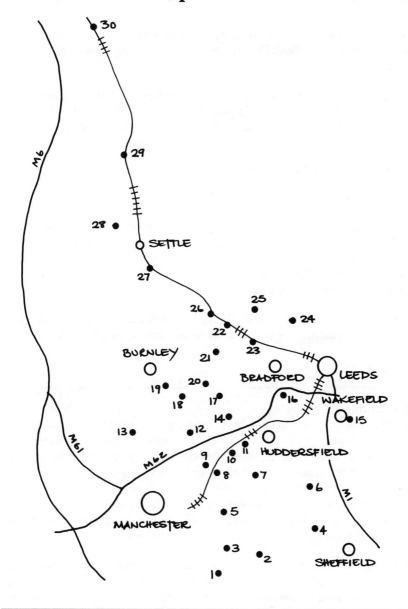

1. WHALEY BRIDGE

A short walk between the Whaley Bridge and Buxworth along the tranquil waters of The Peak Forest canal and returning by the mysterious Roosdyche.

Pub: The Navigation, Johnson Street, off Canal Street. Chesters Mild and Boddingtons Bitter. Open Mondays to Saturdays 1100 – 1500 and 1730 – 2300. Sundays 1200 – 1500 and 1900 – 2230 hours. Bar snacks 1200 – 1400.

Start: Whaley Bridge Railway Station.

Distance: 5 miles (8 km).

Map: Ordnance Survey Outdoor Leisure – The Peak District – The Dark Peak.

Public Transport: There is a daily rail service from Buxton and Manchester. Wayfarer ticket available.

By Car: Travel on the A6 to the Whaley Bridge by pass and follow the signs. There is parking near to the railway station or at the bottom of Canal Street.

Whaley Bridge owes its existence to the River Goyt, which attracted small scale mills to the area where farming had previously prevailed. Also, the township grew as a major transhipment point between The Peak Forest Canal and the Cromford and High Peak railway during the 1830s. Parts of the infrastructure remain, the transhipment shed and the railway incline leading to it. In many respects, however, Whaley had become something of a transport network in previous centuries, for many of the old turnpike roads crossed here bringing with them travellers and local inns, of which many still survive.

The aptly named Navigation, however, came with the Peak Forest canal to serve the needs of the thirsty boatmen. It is set back in a little square off Canal Street and hence not always seen from the main road which is at a higher level. This is a friendly pub with one main room surrounding a central bar. It has reminders on the wall of previous times and very often the leisure boatmen of today call in to share a yarn or two over an excellent pint of Boddingtons.

While it attracts many locals, the Navigation welcomes visitors and is well used by ramblers and boaters calling in after a weary day out in the hills or on the water. It is, after all, the first public house encountered when hitting dry land at Whaley Bridge. There are a few seats outside the front and a beer garden. If you happen to venture farther into the town you will not be disappointed with the selection of pubs. Look out for The Shepherd's Arms, which is open from 1130 until 1500 hours; 1900 hours until 2300 hours on Mondays to Saturdays and usual Sunday times. This traditional Marston's house, at one time a farm house, welcomes walkers in its stone flagged tap room with wooden tables and fireside seats.

The Navigation, Whaley Bridge

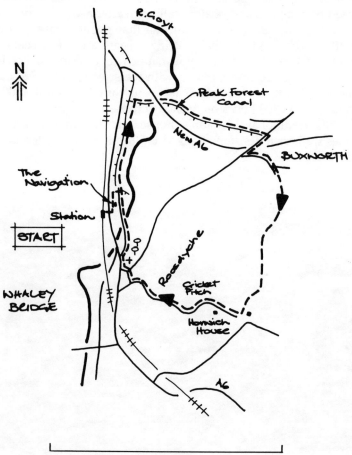

Scale: 1 mile/1.6 Km

Peak Forest Canal

From Whaley Bridge Railway Station pass by the Jodrell Arms to the main road. Cross over and walk down Canal Street by the off licence and fish and chip shop to pass The Navigation. Continue around the corner to the old terminus of the Peak Forest Canal, now a place to hire boats or to enjoy a trip out on one of the cruise narrow boats.

Go left at the far end of this building and then cross the sluice channel to join the main towpath. Follow this along the Peak Forest Canal to its junction with the Buxworth branch of the canal. Cross over the footbridge and once on the other side go right to follow this navigation up to the Buxworth Basin. In recent years the canal branch has slowly but surely been brought back to life again. The path leads to the Buxworth Basin. This would have been a very busy inland port at one time with lime, coal and agricultural goods being transhipped between the canal and the Peak Forest Tramway. The restoration work continues and soon the workplace of the last century will become an inland leisure destination of the next.

Buxworth

Buxworth used to be named Bugsworth after a Norman lord, 'Bugges'. The residents in the 1920s became so fed up with the jibes that they petitioned to Parliament to change the village name with success. However, the magazine 'Punch' got hold of the story and publicised the episode in a very satirical way for some time after. Needles to say, many people still pronounce the 'g' as if the nothing had happened half a century ago.

The towpath leads to a road and to the left is another Navigation pub, which serves Websters' beers. If not calling, go right over the main road and then turn first left. Pass by houses on the right and the road bends to the right. At the next corner look for a track ahead leading to the side of the houses as the road curves left.

This brings you to a gate in a field and by the scars of an old quarry. Skirt these at first but then regain a path climbing up the field with the wall on your right.

Roosdyche

This comes to a stile. Cross it and join a track at a bend. Take the higher fork and climb over the brow to approach a few houses. Cross a stile on the right at this point and walk ahead, following the field's edge to another stile by a gate with the secluded Horwich House to your left. Follow the track to the left of the cricket pitch and shortly afterwards, you will see the Roosdyche on your right. This dry gap looks as if it has been carved naturally by ice, but some theories suggest it that exists because of human kind, possibly being a track for chariot racing or other Roman sport.

The track soon joins another coming in from the right. Continue down the hill a short distance but cut down a walled path right towards the church. Join another lane and turn left and then at the next junction right. Within a matter of a few paces go right again down the old Cromford and High Peak Railway incline down to the transhipment centre at the canal. Turn left for The Navigation and Whaley Bridge Railway station, for there must surely be time for a pint before catching the train home.

2. EDALE

A challenge which comes in two parts: the climb up to Rushup Edge and then the extended route to Sparrowpit. The views of Edale are exquisite.

Pub: The Rambler at Edale. Draught beers from the Scottish and Newcastle range including Theakston's best bitter. Open: Mondays to Saturdays 1900 – 2300. Only open Wednesday, Thursday and Saturday lunchtimes in Winter from 1200 – 1500 hours. Sunday 1200 – 1500. The pub has an arrangement with The Nag's Head at the top of the village so that when one is closed, the other is open. In Summer, it is open every day, lunchtimes and evenings.

The walk also features The Wanted Inn at Sparrowpit serving Robinson's beers. Open: Mondays to Fridays 1100 – 1500 hours and 1730 – 2300. In the summer these hours are often extended from 1100 – 2300. Sundays 1200 – 1500, 1900 – 22.30.

Start: Edale railway station

Distance: To Rushup Edge and return, 8 miles (13 km); to include Sparrowpit 14 miles (22 km)

Map: Ordnance Survey Outdoor Leisure, Series number 1. The Peak District – Dark Peak Area

By Public Transport: There is a daily rail service from Manchester and Sheffield calling at Edale.

By Car: Travel on the A625 from Chapel-en-le-Frith towards Castleton and turn left as signed or by way of Hope from the Sheffield direction looking for the signed Edale road. There is a car park and toilets near to Edale railway station.

The Rambler Inn was known at one time as the Church Inn and the Church Hotel, evidence of which can still be seen on the gable end as you walk away from the station. Its clientele these days is more likely to have come from the railway station than the church, however.

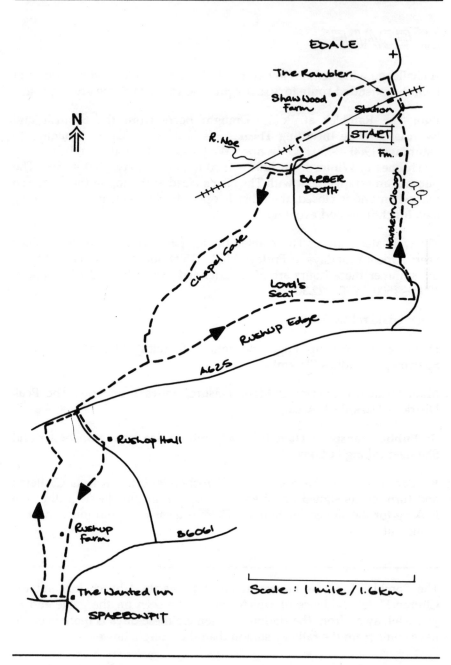

EDALE

The Rambler

Shaw Wood Farm

Station

R. Noe

START

Fm.

BARBER BOOTH

Hardern Clough

Chapel Gate

Lord's Seat

RUSHUP EDGE

A625

Rushop Hall

B6061

Rushup Farm

The Wanted Inn

SPARROWPIT

Scale : 1 mile / 1.6km

The Rambler is often the first stepping off point for those seeking to walk the Pennine Way. It serves a good pint of Theakstons, and food to set a walker off on an intrepid trek. It was once owned by The Ramblers Association but they relinquished it several years ago to the free trade. It caters for locals and visitors alike, and offers accommodation. A few years ago it hosted British Rail's launch of their scenic line guides with personality, Dr David Bellamy. Several TV companies and press photographers turned up, only to find the entire valley shrouded in thick mist as Dr Bellamy stepped off the train. But they interviewed him at close quarters in the pub and a good time was had by all.

Edale

From the railway station, walk off the platform, to the road leading into the village. Those arriving from Sheffield will find a café near the entrance. Turn left and walk past the Rambler inn (later, perhaps). Head towards Edale church (and the Peak Park Information Centre) and at the first corner, as the road curves right, turn left by Champion House. The path is signed along the track but go over a stile on the left and then turn right through a small field to cross another stile.

The walk on this part of the route is well worn and the farmer has waymarked the route with paint and notices in places. Keep ahead for another field, cross a stile by a gate and keep ahead through a field to a gap stile. Once through, head slightly left to a marked tree and cross the track, another stile and a footbridge. Shaw Wood farm is to your right. Head slightly left across the next field and then cross a stile. Keep straight on for a short distance to go over a wooden stile and then through a gap stile just ahead. Walk through this field to a track.

Barber Booth

Go through a white kissing gate, turn left over the railway bridge and onto a road. Turn right and follow this by Barber Booth stores down to the main road. Go over the bridge and turn right along a lane with the River Noe flowing beneath to your right. In a short distance look for a stile on the left. The path follows at first the left bank of a trickle of a stream and then cuts across to the right bank. Cross the stile, go over the track to cross another stile and with the crumbling farm to your left head for the right hand corner of the breeze block enclosure.

Cross the stile by this building and walk the perimeter with a stream on your right. Cross another stile and then keep company with the hedge on your right until another stile is reached. Follow the track ahead as it begins to climb slightly left. Cut right to go over a stile and then head up the field to a stile by a gate. Once over, turn right and now the climbing really begins. The views are worth it, for the fine ridges of Mam Tor and Back Tor can be seen as well as the isolated valley homesteads beneath.

Chapel Gate

This track is known as Chapel Gate and has been popular with ramblers for decades. Pass a Peak District and Northern Footpath Preservation sign dating from 1930 and continue to climb on this main track until a junction is reached. Go right here and follow the track to the main road. Walk for a short distance to the junction. Cross over and turn left down the narrow lane. As the lane begins to descend, there is a stone step stile on the right opposite Rushup Hall.

Head slightly left across the field to a stile which is not clearly identified at first. It is just to the right of a junction of another field boundary. Cross the stile and keep ahead to cross another. Sparrowpit can be seen in the distance across the rough ground that lies between here and this isolated hamlet. In the next field keep ahead with the drystone wall to your right. Cross a stone stile and then a wooden stile and then aim slightly left through wet ground and a broken wall to cross a stile. Head slightly left up the field to cross a further stile with a barn belonging to Rushup farm now firmly in sight.

Proceed to the track to the left of the barn and turn right to walk up the drive to the farmhouse. Please pass with due consideration. Your way is ahead but to the left almost opposite the front door along a narrow path in the garden and cross the stile to exit into a field. Keep ahead and cross a stile into the next field. Head for the gateway to the right of the farm buildings in the field corner. This leads into the farmyard on your left. Walk through it to exit onto the road by the Wanted Inn.

The Wanted Inn used to belong to the Duke of Devonshire's estate and, not surprisingly, was called The Devonshire Arms! When the Duke sought to relinquish this seventeenth century coach house from his estate no one seemed to be interested. After two years or so, a couple bought the pub and named it 'The Wanted Inn' to celebrate the fact. The pub sells Robinsons Best Mild and Best Bitter on electric pump, offers food whenever open. There is one bar serving several areas which were previously separate rooms. The walls are adorned with pictures of local climbs and ridges some of which may be familiar to you now.

Sparrowpit

From the Wanted Inn, turn right and keep ahead along a lane rising out of the hamlet which used to be known as Spar Row. Some of the cottages on the right used to be stables and most of them were then used to house local miners who worked a spar pit across the road, hence the name Spar-row-pit. Just past the last cottage and before a large farm go right and right again along a track. This climbs gently and curves left to a stile. Cross this with care for its construction is poor. Walk ahead along a wide green lane until a stone gateway is reached.

Once through head slightly left across a rough pasture to the far left corner. There is no clear path but look for a barred gate leading onto the main road. Go through the stile by it and turn right to walk facing the traffic. You may notice the tower on the moorland toward to Toot hill. This is a ventilation shaft for the Cowburn tunnel on the Sheffield to Manchester railway line.

Lord's Seat

Walk past the road junction and soon afterwards cross the road and retrace your steps along the old track leading back up to Rushup Edge. At the next junction proceed ahead, however, along Rushup Edge. At first, the views are limited but it soon opens up with exceptional viewpoints, including one known as Lord's Seat, over Edale. Follow this path to the main Edale road. It curves down off the edge to a barred gate. Go left here along a link path through hummocky ground to meet the road farther down. Cross the road and turn left to walk a short distance before crossing a stile on the right. Cross it and bear left down a wet gully. The path winds its way down to a ladder stile and then through a wood in Hardern Clough.

The path leads to a lane. Go straight on by the farm and down to Edale. Notice the National Trust re-planting exercises in this vicinity. At the road junction go right and then next left for Edale once again.

3. HAYFIELD

In the foothills of Kinder Scout, this walk climbs away westwards to the
little hamlet of Rowarth returning by the Sett Valley Trail. A walk with
several climbs.

Pub: The Little Mill, Rowarth. Banks's, Batemans, Hansons and
Robinsons draught ales on sale. Opening Times: Open 1100 – 2300
Mondays to Saturdays and on Sundays at the usual opening times, but
all day for food. Bar snacks at lunchtime and a restaurant in the evening.

Start: Hayfield Bus Station

Distance: 8 miles (13 km)

Map: Outdoor Leisure Map No 1 – The Peak District, Dark Peak Area

Public Transport: Hayfield enjoys a daily service from Stockport on the
bus. This connects with trains from Stockport and Buxton from New
Mills (Newtown) Those coming in from Manchester Piccadilly or
Sheffield alight at New Mills central station, which is five minutes walk
from New Mills Bus Station where the bus to Hayfield can be caught.
There is a less frequent service from Glossop which runs on Mondays to
Saturdays and Summer Sundays. Wayfarer ticket available.

By Car: Travel by way of A6015 off the A6 or the A624 between Glossop
and Chapel-en-le-Frith. There is parking at Hayfield Bus station.

Start at the bus station, the eastern end of The Sett Valley Trail.
Ironically, this used to the terminus of the railway, long since gone. The
buildings are used to house an information centre and toilet block.
Nearby is the cycle hire centre with many a group of cyclists hurtling off
down the trail to New Mills on this traffic free route.

From the bus stop turn right and walk to a gap in the fence to cross the
main road which splits the village in two and is visually intrusive on the
landscape. More importantly at this juncture, take a good look before
crossing as cars speed along it. Once over, walk by the restaurant and

Bulls Head public house to the old road. The fine old church on the left stands by the River Sett, the reason for the existence of the village. This fast flowing river became the power source for many water driven mills throughout the valley and Hayfield became an important centre in this respect.

Hayfield main street

Mass Trespass

One hundred years later it is better known as the walkers' gateway to the massif of Kinder Scout, Bleaklow and Edale Moor. It was also the gathering point for the famous Mass Trespass in 1932 which brought the issue of rights of way to the forefront in the political agenda. There have been celebrations of the event since in Hayfield.

Turn left and follow the road through the village and shortly bear left into Swallow House lane. Go under the main road and then come to another junction. Turn right, passing a telephone kiosk and letter box to

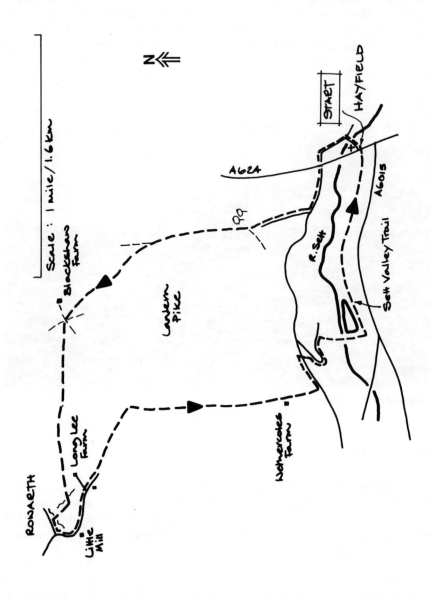

walk up a 'No Through Road'. The lane comes to an end at two buildings. Keep ahead to pass to the right of Primrose cottage and over the footbridge. Climb the walled path through woodland and join a wider track coming in from the left.

Lantern Pike

Continue ahead but at the fork go left, climbing gently once again to pass old farm buildings and onto another house. Pass by it and choose the path rising more steeply left, with views over an old mill, now residential and to the hamlet of Little Hayfield which happens to have a fine little pub, The Lantern Pike. This pub used to be known as the New Inn but was re named to reflect the importance of the hill to your left, Lantern Pike, now owned by the National Trust. The Pike, is said to have been the location for the lighting of beacons in previous times to warn people from miles around of invading armies. Historians suggest that a great bonfire would have been part of a national chain of beacons, lit at the time of the Spanish Armada for example and probably on many other wartime occasions.

Climb up to a stile which is crossed and then turn right. Keep company with the wall to your right and come to a walkers' crossroads. Go left, but not immediately left, over a drystone wall into a field just to your left and signed to Long Lee and Rowarth. Head diagonally across the field through rough grass to meet a drystone wall which should be followed into the dip, which is often wet, and up the bank. However, as the wall curves left your way is ahead over a collapsed section where the stone stile presumably once stood.

Long Lee

Keep ahead over the brow of the hillock and to a gateway in the next boundary. Keep straight on again to a gateway in a field corner and ahead in a similar direction through two further gateways as the ancient farmstead of Long Lee is approached. Pass the Peak District and Northern Counties Footpath Preservation Society's signpost, dated 1926 and built to last. These footpath signs are very much part of rural vernacular architecture hereabouts. Go right in this next field with the farm standing ahead, to follow the wall on the right around to the top far right corner. Exit by a gateway and walk by the barns down the hill and then cut left to a ladder stile over a ditch and wall.

Climb the bank and turn right to walk a short distance to a footbridge over a stream. Cross the bridge and walk to a lane. Turn left here and join another lane to the Little Mill. The pub does not look so little and it was originally a candlewick mill. In the gardens is an old carriage known as The Derbyshire Bell and there are swings *et al* for the children, and seats surrounding the pub.

Inside there is one main room, other than the restaurant/function areas which is broken up into several nooks. The walls are adorned with old pictures and notices including one which reads:

'It is forbidden for vagrants, beggars, itinerant musicians and females of doubtful reputation to enter these premises . . . By Order' May 1901. It says a good deal about the values at the turn of the century and about the state of the economy.

The large fireplace adds to the setting and at the bar is a range of draught beers which vary but usually includes Banks's and Hansons ales on handpull.

From the entrance to the pub turn right and continue along the 'No Through Road'. This peters out at a farmstead and becomes a rough track, climbing up at first and then straightening on the moorland with fine views across the Sett Valley. Pass Wethercotes farm with old vehicles and agricultural implements strewn all around the track. Soon after a lane is reached. Turn left and walk a short distance passing a building on the left before going right as signposted down a gorse clad ban' Your way is slightly right to exit from the field by a U bend in the lane.

Go left here to head down the lower track and as you approach the house look for a stile on the right and proceed down the field ahead towards the reservoir. Go through a gate and follow the well worn path down the bank and over a bridge. Turn left and walk along the dam. The path joins the Sett Valley Trail. Turn left for the gentlest part of the walk to Hayfield.

4. LOW BRADFIELD

A short walk between the villages of Upper and Lower Bradfield in the south eastern foothills of the Pennine range. Bradfield parish council have done a splendid job in maintaining and waymarking where necessary paths in their locality.

Pub: The Haychatter, Bradfield Dale. A variety of guest beers. Open Monday to Sunday 1930 – 2300 but opening times tend to be a little erratic in Winter. Open Sunday lunchtimes 1200 – 1400.

Start: From Smithy Bridge Road, Lower Bradfield

Distance: 5 miles (8 km)

Map: Pathfinder Sheet 726, Sheffield and Stocksbridge. Landranger Sheet 110, Sheffield and Huddersfield area.

Public Transport: There is a daily bus service (61) from Sheffield

By Car: From Sheffield travel on the B6077 to Loxley and Low Bradfield. From Derbyshire travel on the A57 from Glossop and then take the Strines turning on the left after Ladybower. Follow this road over Strines Moor, to pass the Strines Inn and then after Bole Edge plantation turn right for Low Bradfield.

The Haychatter, an unusual name for a public house, is situated on a back road between Low Bradfield and Strines in Bradfield Dale. It is a most unlikely survivor particularly as there is also a pub in Low Bradfield, another in High Bradfield and the enterprising Strines Inn further up the road which will serve you a coffee in the morning.

The Haychatter provides a variety of cask conditioned beers to serve by handpull with such delights as Adnams, Batemans, Burton Bridge and Old Mill so there's always a surprise awaiting the walker. There are three rooms but the main bar, often with an open fire blazing in Winter, is most popular. There's no doubt that the pub comes into its own during summer months when it is much busier. More's the pity that it does not open lunchtimes or at least on Saturday mid-day.

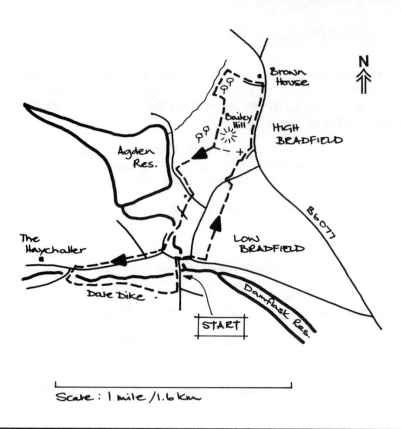

Scale : 1 mile / 1.6 km

Bradfield

Start from the bridge on Smithy Road bridge. Walk ahead to the garage and turn right along the road signed to Loxley. Within a very short distance look for steep stone steps rising on the left into a field. Walk up this field keeping company with a drystone wall on your right and go over stone steps and ahead again up the hill towards the impressive church of High Bradfield. The view back over to Damflask reservoir is marvellous, so take a breather to admire this beautiful stretch of water.

Keep in the same direction over a broken wall and soon cross another two stone stiles, straight on in the direction of the church. This stands on an impressive site, dating from mediaeval times but mainly form the fifteenth century including several fine stained glass windows.

Body Snatchers

Follow the field's edge to a stone stile in the far corner and exit onto a road. Turn right and, at the corner, cross over. Go over the stone step stile and a wooden stile. Turn left to walk up the field to the churchyard. Go through the green gate to walk along a perimeter path with brings you to the main entrance to the church and a road. On your left is the old 'Watch House', at one time a caretaker's house. The incumbent would look out for body snatchers. Unless calling at the Old Horns public house (Whitbread) keep ahead up Jane Street. At the next junction turn left.

Walk along the lane until you reach a house on the left. The path is on the left through a white gate and between bushes in an outer part of the

The church at High Bradfield

garden which leads to a walled green lane. Cross the stile and descend by a coniferous wood, through a kissing gate and down to a corner where you turn left. The path follows a parallel line to the Roche End Brook well below on the right but shortly turn left and then left through a kissing gate to walk up a dark canopy between trees. This short section illustrates convincingly the way in which conifers like these squeeze out plant and wildlife.

Flood

Walk between two stone gateway posts and turn right. The path begins to climb gently along the edge of Bailey Hill through deciduous woodland. The hill is thought to have been the site of a motte and bailey castle, hence the name. Earthworks still remain but they are difficult to discern in the wood. There are, however, superb views through the trees of Agden reservoir. The construction of these reservoirs in the last century must have been a formidable engineering task and not without risk. In 1864 Dale Dike partly collapsed and the floods killed 24 people in the lower reaches of the Loxley valley as a torrential wave of water hit villages and homesteads during the dead of night.

Before reaching the stile leading to the church go right and the path descends to the road by the reservoir. Turn left and after a short distance look for a path on the right just beyond a house on the right. The walled path soon crosses a track and then leads down steps to a river. At the time of writing a minor diversion was in hand at this point. Thus, the waymark could advise you to cross the bridge and turn left. On the other hand, you might have to make a slight diversion by turning left before the river and within fifty or sixty paces go over another footbridge on your right. Either way you come to a track by a children's playground which leads up to Fair House Lane.

Folly

Turn right and keep ahead when passing the bus turning point. On this section of the walk, you might catch a glimpse of a tower on the moors to your left. This is a folly built to encourage local employment in times of sever depression. On Bradfield moor, there is a similar tower, known as Boot's Folly after its sponsor, Charles Boot. At the next junction take the lower fork unless visiting the Haychatter public house which is the right fork and just around the corner. Your route, however, leads over the bridge and as the lane begins to climb, just before a junction to the riding school, look for a stile on the left.

Cross the step stile and walk ahead above the scrub and river below. You reach a stone stile which is crossed and the well worn path leads ahead again to a stile by a gate. Join the track which passes by a cottage and into Bradfield.

The track comes to a road. Turn left to pass by the Plough and to Smithy Bridge Road. Notice the map of walks in the parish on the noticeboard. What more could the walker ask for?

5. HADFIELD

Pleasant walking country in and around reservoirs in the lower reaches of the Woodhead valley near the small Derbyshire town of Hadfield. There are no real climbs on this walk.

Pub: The Palatine Hotel, Hadfield. Mon-Sat 1300 (Noon on Sat) to 2300 hours; Sundays 1200 – 1500 and 1900 – 2230.

Distance: 6 miles (10 km)

Map: Ordnance Survey Outdoor Leisure Map No. 1 – The Peak District – The Dark Peak

Public Transport: There is a frequent train service from Manchester Piccadilly to Hadfield. Contact 061 832 8353. There are also several buses. Contact Derbyshire Busline (0298) 23098.

By Car: Hadfield is signposted from the main A57 road out of the East Manchester and the A628 from Sheffield.

Hadfield was known to the Romans as a strategic point on the route across the Pennines and has been a calling point for travellers ever since. It is no more than a small industrial town these days with an increasing number of residents dependent on travelling to Manchester for employment. They are, of course, very fortunate in that they can escape in their leisure time to the hills of Longdendale for the area offers fine walking without crowds.

Start the walk from Hadfield railway station, no more than a platform now, but once a relatively important stop on the Woodhead line between Manchester and Sheffield. It was this railway which encouraged the building of larger mills and factories in the area during the last century. British Railways decided, however, that the number of routes across the Pennines had to be reduced and despite a vigorous campaign against the closure the line beyond Hadfield closed. The station buildings have had a reprieve and house a ticket office and public house-cum-restaurant.

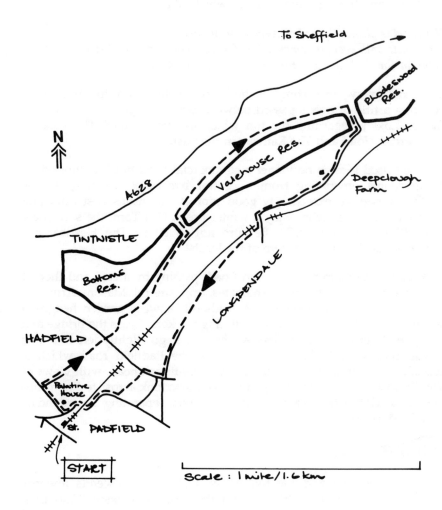

At the bottom of the Station approach stands the Palatine Hotel which at one time was a coaching inn. It used to be featured in several Victorian directories and touring guides one of which states:

'The Hotel is pleasantly and conveniently situated
And replete with every accommodation for the Commercial gentleman.
Agent for Smith, Nephews...Brewers-Worksop and Retford'

There are many interesting plaques and pictures on the pub walls including a title of deeds passed between Lord Howard of Glossop and Charles Loxley regarding the inn which has been called The Palatine Commercial Hotel and The Railway in the past.

This well used local is no longer a commercial hotel but the dimensions of the rooms emanating from a central bar reflect its origins. The landlord serves an exceedingly good pint of Robinsons Best Mild and Bitter and for those who enjoy a winter brew, Old Tom, the sort of ale which blots out brain cells. Be sure not to sit in The Headbangers Corner, set aside for one or two of the locals!

Walk down the main road, Station Road, passing by a café and then at the first turn, go right along Lambgates, opposite the Masons Arms. At the end of this short street a path leads off between garden hedges, a path which is obviously popular with dog walkers. Cross the bridge and keep ahead along a field hedge. At the corner go slightly left to a stile leading into a track. This brings you to the Padfield road which is crossed. Go through an unusual stile and continue ahead, with views of Woodhead now beginning to open up. You also look across to Robinsons Moss and Tintwistle Knarr, bleak moorlands separating Longdendale from Saddleworth.

Bottoms

Cross another stile and the follow the path as it descends towards Bottoms Reservoir, the settlement on the other side being Tintwistle. Cross a stile and join a path alongside the dry stone wall and go forward along it until a road is reached. Go left along the dam but at the far end turn right to follow a concessionary path along the route of a dismantled railway. This is Valeshouse reservoir, longer than Bottoms but not as large as Torside and Woodhead farther up the valley.

This section is pleasant enough but do watch out for the joggers as they speed past on their second or third lap around the reservoir. The road eventually leads up the top of the dam, (although the fit will go for the short cut steps), holding back Rhodeswood Reservoir, a rather scenic water landscape sandwiched between Torside and Valehouse.

Woodhead Line

Turn right and walk along the dam and then follow the track as it bears right climbing gently to Deepclough farm. Keep ahead on the now tarmac lane as it winds left to cross the old Woodhead line, soon to become a Trans Pennine walking and cycling route. What a splendid re use of a sadly neglected resource.

At the other side of the bridge look sharp for your way is over a stile on the right and down to a stream. Once over, go through the gap stile ahead and proceed slightly left through a field to a gateway. Keep ahead in a similar direction and you soon come to a junction of tracks. Keep slightly left, then go through a gap stile by a gateway and thus join a track which leads up to the village of Padfield.

Padfield

The track exits onto a main street in Padfield, a much quieter village these days with few surviving mills. Turn right, and walk through the village. The Peel Arms is glimpsed to your left and soon you are at the outskirts on the Padfield Main Road. Cross the road and look for a gap stile on the left. This leads through a field, by a smallholding and exits by garages onto another road. Turn right and walk along the pavement for the short distance into Hadfield.

6. DENBY DALE TO PENISTONE

A walk along old bridleways and packhorse tracks between West and South Yorkshire

Pub: The Old Crown, Penistone. Tetley Bitter. Open Mondays, Tuesdays and Wednesdays 1100 – 1500, Thursdays 1630, Saturdays 1530. Evenings 1900 – 2300, but Sundays 2230.

Start: Denby Dale Station

Distance: 5 miles (8 km)

Maps: Pathfinder Sheet 715; Landranger Sheet 110

Public Transport: hourly (Sundays two-hourly); train (Metro Train) on the Penistone Line from Huddersfield or Sheffield (BR Table 34). Metro Day Rover valid from Huddersfield to Denby Dale; pay excess on return from Penistone.

By Car: Park at Penistone station, catch train to Denby Dale, walk back to car.

One of the delights of this walk is to travel the little known (outside Yorkshire) but picturesque Penistone railway line, with its considerable number of viaducts and tunnels and extensive views.

Leave Denby Dale station by the southern (Penistone) end, going through the tunnel under the tracks and following the path left. Along the embankment a track leads under the huge, curving Denby Dale viaduct. This handsome viaduct was built in 1882 to replace a wooden structure on the old Lancashire and Yorkshire railway, and is 112 feet high above the valley floor.

Immediately before the viaduct take an opening down steps, right, to the main A636 road. Cross it and continue down the path parallel to the viaduct which descends steps and runs alongside a factory fence, over a stream, before climbing to join another path and cobbled way up to the A635 Barnsley Road.

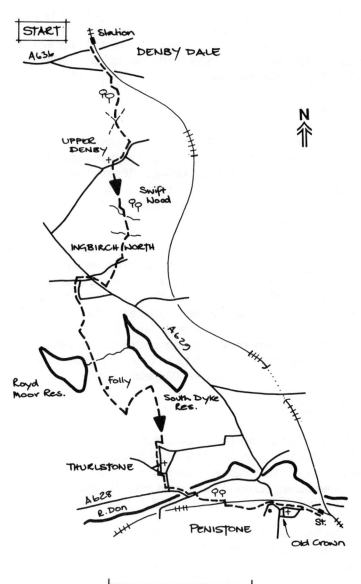

START

☦ Station

DENBY DALE

A636

UPPER
DENBY

Swift
Wood

INGBIRCH (NORTH

N

A629

Royd
Moor Res.

Folly

South Dyke
Res.

THURLSTONE

A628

R. Don

PENISTONE

St.

Old Crown

Scale : 1 mile / 1.6 km

Cross and almost directly opposite you'll see a bridleway sign and a track curving into a wood. This becomes an enclosed way between stone walls which soon bears left and begins to ascend through attractive deciduous woods, at first parallel with the railway, with fine views across the village of Denby Dale.

Denby Dale

Denby Dale's greatest claim to fame lies in gigantic meat pies – the biggest in the world, only baked on special occasions. This tradition began in 1788 to celebrate king George III's recovery from mental breakdown. The one baked in 1964 weighed 6.5 tons and was cooked in a dish 18 feet long. The last pie was cooked in 1987 and the dish still stands outside the village.

The path swings right and gradually reaches a summit. It eventually levels out and reaches a crossing of paths. Your way is straight ahead indicated by a footpath sign, through a tall stone squeezer stile which leads into a field. Follow the hedge on the left of the field to the houses ahead, to the left of which the path continues into an alleyway. Keep ahead to where this path joins a back lane, Coal Pit Lane, in Upper Denby, where you turn right into the centre of the village by a post office and narrow green with a bench. Turn right again into the lane, and walk towards the church about 300 metres ahead.

Swift Wood

Just before the church and the school, cross to where a bridleway, left, signed Ingbirchworth branches off left to a bridlegate. The way bears left between a rather hostile barbed wire fence and the wall. It follows the edge of a field before becoming a sunken track alongside a beck, dipping into a little wood of tall trees, Swift Wood, still by the streamside.

The track bridges the stream and leaves the wood at a gate. Your way is directly ahead, up a knoll and alongside holly trees and fieldside fence, before dipping again into an attractive little ravine with a footbridge and bridlegate. Cross, climbing the other side across a field corner to another gate, where as blue waymarks indicate, you turn sharply left alongside the wall. Keep ahead through the next bridlegate, but where the path enters a broad crossing track which lies between twin wooden fences, turn right for about 100 metres to a wooden stile in the fence to your left. Cross, and make your way diagonally along a clear path across the field to a stone stepstile by the field corner and gateway. Cross the next narrow field to another step stile directly ahead, and a path which leads behind garages to the main A629 Sheffield road at Ingbirchworth.

Lions

Turn right along this road through the village, but where the main road swings right, look for a narrow lane forking down to the left, Mill Lane. Less than 100 metres along this lane, turn left into a second lane, High Lane, and climb past a house with handsome medieval-looking lions guarding its gatepost.

At the T-junction ahead, turn right but almost on the corner between a house and a farm runs another enclosed bridlepath, left, clearly marked with a sign. Follow this very pleasant way between stone walls, almost running southwards between fields. After about 300 metres it turns sharp left, now becoming a more sunken way and descending a little gully below Royd Moor Reservoir dam. The path crosses a footbridge over Maize Brook, and climbs up a stony way between heather up the other side.

At a cottage, the stony path becomes an access track which levels out and continues to a farmhouse called, for enigmatic reasons, Folly. Continue past it and along a tarmac lane for another 400 metres to another junction this time with a signposted grassy track. Turn left here, and follow yet another broad path between field walls as it curves towards South Dyke Reservoir, ending at a gate and stile on the right.

Go through here into an area of open land and scattered woodland ahead following the wall on the right. At the wall corner, several waymarks and a stile indicate the path continuing on the right hand side of the wall ahead. However, most people seem to keep between a gap onto an elevated embankment on the left of the wall. Both routes converge after a couple of fields and lead to a stile in the wall corner on the right by the beck.

Thurlstone

Cross here, turning right parallel with hedge and stream to a gate and stile into another enclosed track on the left. Follow this into the outskirts of Thurlstone where you turn right on a back lane and left leading into and along Thurlstone's main street. Thurlstone is an attractive mixture of old and new, the old weavers' cottages and tall houses in soot-blackened grit, more interesting than the new. Keep straight on as Towngate curves past the Crystal Palace Inn (John Smiths), taking the steps on the left into Manchester Road (A628).

Follow Manchester Road left downhill past the cottages named Tenterfields, and to cross the River Don towards Penistone. Soon past the bridge and the minor road junction on the left, look for a row of cottages on the right forming Stottercliffe Road. Turn right here, keeping left where the track forks, but where you seem to be entering a field at a gateway, take the narrow enclosed footpath sharply left.

Trans Pennine Trail

This path soon enters woodland and crosses a concrete bridge over the trackbed of the much lamented Woodhead railway, the one time electrified Manchester-Sheffield line. This is likely soon to have a new lease of life as the Trans-Pennine Trail from Hull to Liverpool, Britain's first European Long Distance Footpath.

The path swings left and enters a broad open field. Keep straight ahead parallel with the old railway line, heading for the stone buildings ahead. Keep left of these to join a minor road by the Fire Station. Turn left down to the main Manchester road by the railway bridge. Go right up St Mary's Street to the centre of Penistone and into Market Street where you'll find The Old Crown. A comfortable old pub with excellent Tetley's on offer, a choice of lunchtime food and a warm South Yorkshire welcome.

Penistone

Penistone is another of those no-nonsense Pennines towns which still retains an air of importance from its position as a crossing and trading point of the Pennines in early days in the textile industry. Among buildings of interest are a rare late 17th century Dissenter's Chapel, an 18th century Cloth Hall and the fine 15th century church with an impressive tower containing ancestors of the William Wordsworth. Allow at least ten minutes' walk to the station. The quickest way is down Church Street to the left of the Church and up the (long) station drive. The surviving sections of the once grand Great Central Railway station on a triangle between the Manchester and Huddersfield lines, is largely rented out to small business, but the canopy on the Huddersfield platform is supported by some fine wrought iron work in which the insignia MSLR (Manchester Sheffield and Lincoln Railway), predecessor of the Great Central Railway, is visible.

7. THE HOLME VALLEY

Riversides and reservoirs from Yorkshire's Summer Wine Country to the northern edge of the Peak National Park.

Pub: The Fleece, Holme. Theakston's Old Peculiar, XB, Best Bitter, Younger's IPA, 80 shilling, Matthew Brown Mild. Open Monday-Friday, Winter Saturdays 1100 – 1500 and 1900 – 2300; Summer Saturdays 1100 – 2300; Sundays 1200 – 1500 and 1900 – 2230. Food daily when pub is open.

Start: Holmfirth Church

Distance: 10 miles (16 km)

Map: Pathfinder Sheet 714 Holmfirth; Landranger 110, Seffield and Huddersfield area.

Public Transport: Metro Train Huddersfield Line (BR Table 39) to Penistone Line (BR Table 34) then Yorkshire Rider bus 310, 312 to Holmfirth.

By Car: Park in Holmfirth – crowded on summer Sundays.

Fans of Compo, Foggy and Clegg will find much on this walk familiar, given television's ability to endow the ordinary with the power of myth. Reality even follows illusion; the former hardware shop to the right of Holmfirth Church was converted to the Sid's café of the TV series to meet otherwise disappointed expectations.

Holmfirth

Such absurdities apart, Holmfirth is a Pennine town of greater character, in a setting of superb moorland countryside which adds much to the success of the TV series. The town also has its grim side as a plaque on a house wall in the town centre testifies when a tragic flood from a burst reservoir dam last century caused great loss of life. An exhibition about that flood is to be seen in the town's museum, above the library on the

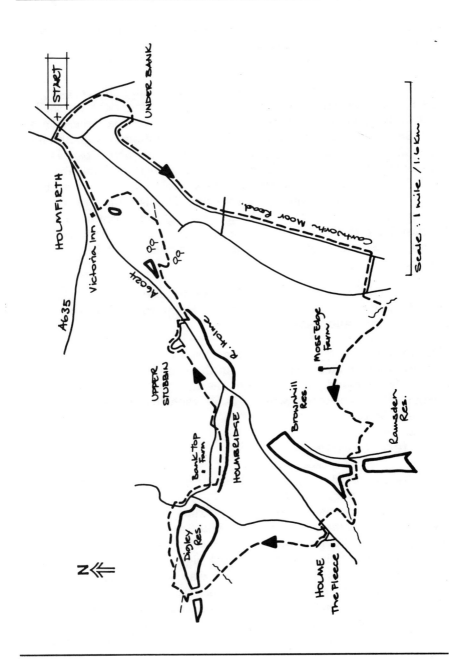

main road. There is also the superb Postcard Museum based around
Bamforth's of Holmfirth, whose fat ladies in swimming costumes with
skinny red-nosed husbands are a part of British seaside folklore.

Start the walk at Holmfirth's lovely eighteenth century church, along the
paved way between Sid's café and Church, turning right up shallow
steps to the road behind. Cross to the second, lower road, the Dunford
road (B6106) and turn left past the Shoulder of Mutton to walk uphill for
about 400 metres. Pass a mill pond on the right to where a part-asphalt,
part-cobbled track drops down to mill buildings at Underbank above the
pond. Immediately past the mill a narrow track, between walls, climbs
out of the little valley through birchwoods. This is soon a grassy way,
curving up to a group of seventeenth and eighteenth century cottages.
Go past these to the right to join a lane. Keep ahead along here, but
almost immediately, on the left, a track curves uphill in front of a
bungalow.

This track curves around the nose of the hill, soon giving spectacular
views back across to the stone rooftops of Holmfirth, and down into the
narrow Holme Valley below.

This track is a stony way, climbing steadily uphill past old quarry
workings and isolated farms. Keep on the main track as it follows the
ridge side farmland on your right, heather on the left. You finally
emerge at a cross-roads with a quiet asphalted farm road ahead,
Cartworth Moor Road.

Wooded Ravine

Walk straight ahead, easy fast walking for almost a mile, past a cricket
ground, and a couple of farms. Beyond the second of these, Moorfield,
the lane becomes unsurfaced again and dips past an old quarry now
covered with heather. You reach a wide, rutted track on the right
between stone walls. Turn right here to reach a lane where just to the left
you'll see a metal field gate by a footpath sign. Follow the wallside path
which soon becomes a delectable green way which curves around the
edge of a shallow, partially wooded ravine. The way is marked by
fieldgates. Keep ahead, through the gates, then follow the field wall
above Moss Edge Farm, beyond which the path takes two smaller
pedestrian gates to enter a walled, grassy track. This now swings left

and heads for the magnificent outline of the Bleakmires, Holme Moss and Black Hill, with the tall mast of Holme Moss TV station a notable landmark.

As the track dips and swings to the right, a path crosses to a tall wooden ladder stile at the edge of the wood ahead, over a little wooden footbridge. Make for and cross the stile, following a track along the right hand side of the wood through a picnic area and emerging at Ramsden Reservoir by the car park.

Brownhill Reservoir

Turn right here, soon reaching the dam between Ramsden and Brownhill Reservoirs where, on the left, you'll see fingerposts and a narrow path between iron fencing which drops down to the dam. Follow the path across the dam, turning right by the outflow alongside Brownhill Reservoir. Cross a low hill to descend another lovely path through heather, bilberry and bluebells (depending on the time of year) to a footbridge by a waterfall across Rake Dike, climbing back up to the right-hand, following the signs to Holme, across a field to where a stile leads to an enclosed path alongside fields and a curious, half sunken 'eco house' – designed with many conservation features by a local architect – on the left before reaching the road. Turn left for about 200 metres to the centre of the village.

The Fleece, a pleasant and comfortable pub, offers a choice of first class Theakston's and Younger's beer and excellent choice of food. There is a homely atmosphere and, considering the pub is as inland as one could find, the regulars participate in events to raise funds for the Royal National Lifeboat Institute several times a year.

Sit outside in warm weather but leave your boots in the porch if wet. The pub is well used to walkers and more often than not you'll find a dog tied up outside or boots lined up outside the front entrance.

If you've walked enough at this point, the hourly Yorkshire Rider 308 bus takes you from almost outside the pub back to Holmfirth and Huddersfield. Otherwise turn right to the broad cobbled square by the bus stop, and make your way to the top end where a narrow lane curves away. Look for a footpath sign by a gate just past a small barn on the right, opposite a cottage known as The Nook.

The Fleece, Holme

Kirklees Way

This path is waymarked with the usual arrows and a blue K indicating the Kirklees Way. It first follows the field wall over stone stiles before crossing a series of fields, bearing slightly to the right. The way is marked by stiles and, as you dip towards Digley Reservoir, footpath signs, before crossing a little footbridge and going through pedestrian gates to the attractive path across the dam between Bilberry and Digley Reservoir.

At the end of the dam turn left into another walled lane, which soon zigzags right. At the junction of tracks ignore waymarks indicating the track left, but keep straight on along the track by the reservoir to follow the edge of the reservoir, soon becoming a footpath along the wall before rejoining a track to the lane. Just before the lane, take the path through the kissing gate on the right, marked by a footpath sign. This goes down steps past the edge of the reservoir (fine views and ample birdlife) emerging close to the edge of the main dam. Turn right to the dam, but don't cross it. Go down the road to follow the main valley downhill for about 100 metres to a point just below the dam, opposite Bank Top farm where a little metal pedestrian gate on the right leads to a path down the embankment. This meets the reservoir access road below the embankment.

Follow this for about 400 metres to where you'll see a narrow track on the left slope steeply up to rejoin the lane above. Take this, turning right, as the lane begin to drop into Holmebridge. Ignore the first path off left but take the second, which runs immediately behind a row of red bridge houses, Holme Close, before the old school. This path begins as a narrow enclosed way, but soon runs alongside the wall between gardens, finally descending towards Upper Stubbin where it swings left to join a track which curves around yet another mill pond. Join the lane and follow it to where, on the left, it meets the main road.

Cross the main road, and continue straight ahead down Coop Street taking the first street on the left. This leads past cottages to Whitley and Green's Mill and then beyond the mill car park to a track between the River Holme and the Mill race. Keep ahead to the next mill with a tall red chimney, about 50 metres from which is a footbridge on the right. Cross, but take the grassy path sharp right which slopes diagonally uphill for 100 metres to where it meets a similar path coming in from the left. Take this to the left, climbing up to the wood on the left which is entered by a stile. The path continues through the woods to where it climbs to a narrow stone gap ahead, a former bridge between stone walls at an old quarry. You join yet another narrow path here. Take it to the left, the path now sloping through woods or birch and beech, eventually coming out of the wood and curving to the left to once again rejoin the A6024.

Facing you is the Victoria Inn, a lovely end-of-the walk pub, as period as its name, offering excellent Timothy Taylors and Tetley Mild and Bitter. You could catch the bus at the stop nearby, otherwise it's about 500 metres back into the centre of Holmfirth. If you are going back by bus remember that most of the buses leave from the bus stop on the main Huddersfield road beyond the town centre cross roads.

8. UPPERMILL

A walk through this increasingly popular area between Uppermill and the outlying hamlet of Diggle in Saddleworth. There are a few climbs but the walking is rewarded by several very good pubs.

Pub: The Diggle Hotel, Diggle. Boddingtons and Oldham Bitter, Oldham Mild, Timothy Taylors Golden Best and Landlord. Open Mondays to Fridays 1200 – 1500 and 1900 – 2300; Saturdays 1200 – 2300; Sunday 1200 – 1500 and 1900 – 2230. Bar food is available every lunch and evening.

Start: Greenfield Railway Station

Distance: 8 miles (13 km)

Map: Pathfinder Sheets 713 Oldham, 714 Holmfirth; Landranger Sheet 109 Manchester and 110 Sheffield and Huddersfield area.

Public Transport: There is an hourly train and bus service from Huddersfield and Manchester to Greenfield. There is also a bus service from Huddersfield, Marsden, Oldham and Manchester to Greenfield and Uppermill. There is a bus service from Diggle to Uppermill if a cut off point is required.

Greenfield was no more than a hamlet in the early nineteenth century but grew up as a cotton milling centre around the waters of the Chew valley. Nearby is Dovestones reservoir, and this waterside recreational facility has become a very popular haunt in recent years. Above the town is the hill top known as 'Pots and Pans', weathered rocks forming a well-known landmark seen from miles around.

From the Greenfield Railway station entrance, go right down the hill by the Railway Hotel and then sharp left to drop down to a bridge over the canal. Go left to join the Huddersfield Canal towpath and keep ahead to walk into Greenfield. Exit in approximately half a mile onto the main High Street in Uppermill with the museum on your left and the Alexandria Mill and Craft Centre on the right, two major visitor attractions in Saddleworth.

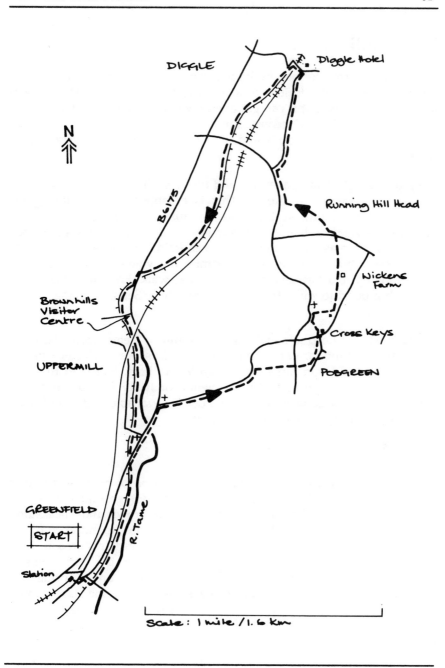

N

DIGGLE

Diggle Hotel

B6175

Running Hill Head

Nickens Farm

Brownhills Visitor Centre

Cross Keys

UPPERMILL

POBGREEN

GREENFIELD

START

R. Tame

Station

Scale : 1 mile / 1.6 Km

Uppermill

Uppermill has transformed in the past ten years or so from being a town which looked a little forlorn to a thriving tourism centre. The price of such popularity is that it can get overcrowded on Sunday afternoons as people come to the craft centre, museum or simply to wander along the main street. There are cafés and a few gift shops, and several public houses.

Keep to the right hand pavement and turn right up New Street which is signed to Saddleworth church. This is a laborious climb taking ten minutes or more but, as the road eventually curves left, look for a footpath between a house and garage on the right. This path soon becomes sunken as it rises higher between field boundaries. Do not walk up the steps but pause awhile to admire the views behind. The main path leads up to a tarmac lane. Cross it and walk through a small piece of rough ground to join a track, known locally as Settstones lane. Go left here.

At the next fork keep left again and come out by Peters Farm. Turn left and descend to the car park entrance of The Cross Keys. This is a superb pub serving mild and bitter from John Willie Lees. Home to the local mountain rescue club and also the venue of lively folk sessions, The Cross Keys has a good atmosphere. Food is available and families are welcome at lunchtime and early evening.

Saddleworth Church

At the far left corner of the car park the path drops towards Saddleworth church and what a fine view including in the foreground the Church Inn, another pleasant hostelry serving Matthew Brown and Theakston's beers. If sober after these two stops, turn right to the entrance of the church, dating from the thirteenth century but much restored in later centuries. This church reflects the importance of the early hillside settlements, often referred to as folds. It was only during the mid-nineteenth century that the valley settlements gained ascendancy with the rise of steam powered mills, rows of cottages and the beginnings of mass transport.

Oldham Way

Turn right, skirting the churchyard, and then passing through a farmyard as the track rises. At the corner just beyond, cross the stile and turn left to walk along the remains of a wall to cross another stile. Keep ahead as the Oldham Way markers indicate, to pass beneath the ruins of Wickens farm. Join an old green track through Wickens Clough and climb up to go through a small stone gateway on the right hand side of the bank. Keep ahead along the top of the clough, heading across the field to a ladder stile. Cross this, turn left on the lane and, in a short distance,look for a track off to the right as signposted, down a track known as Hill Barn lane. This is part of the Oldham Way, a circular walk through the borough of Oldham, becoming increasingly popular with walkers.

This track exits onto a tarmac road. Go right and follow it to a triangular junction where the right fork is taken. The road soon leads into Diggle passing old works on the right and then up to the green with The Diggle Hotel ahead. Diggle grew up as a small fold but then gained greater significance as the last call before climbing Standedge along a packhorse route or in later years through one of the Standedge tunnels by canal or train. There used to be a station at Diggle and what a pity it is not reopened today for residents and visitors.

The Diggle Hotel

The Diggle Hotel was built to serve such trade and the building of the pub is celebrated every May Day with Beer Drinking contests, entertainment and fun as the pictures over the bar illustrate. The bar serves three separate areas in the pub, one including a side room and the food is well appreciated by customers. There are several ornaments and pictures decorating the walls, including a series of owl ceramics, a centenary plate and old coins. It all adds to the character of this house but above all else the beer is beautiful. A civilised touch is that coffee is also served at most times!

Diggle Flight

Cross the bridge over the railway, turn left and at the next corner keep ahead along the towpath of the Huddersfield Canal. Pass by Worth Mills and then Dobcross Loom works. The path comes to the main road over the top, known as the 'Woolroad' as so much wool would have been transported from the hill farms to producers along this early turnpike road. Cross over to re join the towpath, passing by the old transshipment shed and then around to the Brownhills Visitor Centre. Pass under the skewed bridge of the Saddleworth viaduct and onto the museum at Uppermill and railway station at Greenfield.

9. DELPH

A ramble from the busy village of Delph to Heights and Castleshaw across bleak moorland and by a feeder stream of the River Tame.

Pub: The Royal Oak Inn, Heights, Delph. Chesters Mild and a variety of bitters on rotation – Bentleys Yorkshire, Boddingtons, Castle Eden, Flowers, Marstons Pedigree, Ruddles County and other guest beers! Open Monday to Fridays 1900 – 2300, Saturday and Sunday 1200 – 1500; 1900 – 2300 hours. Home cooked food available including local game in season. No sandwiches or chips!

Start: The Rose and Crown, by Delph Bridge.

Distance: 8 miles (13 km)

Map: Pathfinder Sheet 713 Oldham. Landranger 109 Manchester.

Public Transport: There are regular buses from Manchester, Oldham and Uppermill and Hyde. Contact Greater Manchester Passenger Transport on 061 226 8181 for details. The Hyde to Delph bus passes Greenfield railway station which offers an hourly service to and from Manchester and Huddersfield.

By Car: Travel on the A62 from Huddersfield to Oldham, turning off for Delph village at Delph Crossroads. Alternatively, travel on the A672 to Denshaw and then turn onto the A6052 to Delph. There is limited parking in the village.

Delph has become fashionable in recent years and this has had an inevitable impact on the village. This trend, however, has kept many retail premises going which would have otherwise vanished. The village dates mainly from the mid eighteenth century and many of the buildings huddled around the old turnpike road and River Tame are there because of wool production.

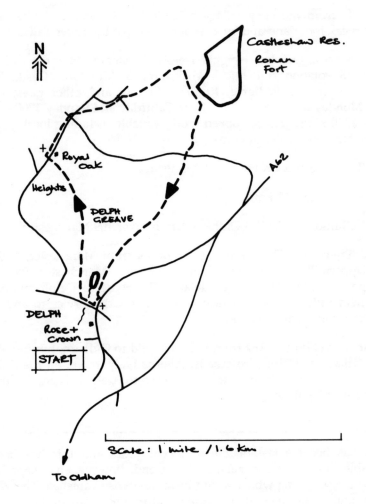

N

Castleshaw Res.
Roman Fort

A62

Royal Oak

Heights

DELPH GREAVE

DELPH

Rose + Crown

START

Scale: 1 mile / 1.6 Km

To Oldham

Delph Donkey

One hundred years later, a single track railway arrived leaving the Huddersfield and Manchester railway near to Saddleworth viaduct. This peculiar little railway was know throughout its hundred year existence as The Delph Donkey, not only because it was originally horse-drawn but also because of its very slow pace during the days of steam. In the 1980s a brief feasibility study was undertaken to see if the Donkey could be re-introduced as a tourism proposition but the proposal came to nothing.

Sunday lunchtimes can become unpleasant in these parts as a stream of cars pass through the village centre so avoid this leisure based rush hour if possible. At other times, Delph settles to a less frenetic pace and Saturday is an excellent day to enjoy this ramble.

From The Rose and Crown, turn left to walk up to a cross roads. Go left into Denshaw Road but very shortly go right, once past the brook, up a narrow tarmac road (signposted 'No Through Road'). This climbs away from the houses, offering views of Delph and the Tame Valley. The path passes just to the left of the houses, rising as a green track with the wall to your right. The track shortly crosses the wall and for the remaining stretch up to The Royal Oak Inn, follow the wall which is now on your left.

Friarmere

This isolated public house, standing opposite St Thomas's church, was at one time the centre of an area known as Friarmere when the population living and working in the hills was far greater than today. The inn, often referred to by the locals as " Th' Heights" is mentioned in Ammon Wrigley's dialect poem "Owd Donty's Supperin Do". This well known local poet was a frequent visitor to the inn, no doubt seeking inspiration for his writing. His memorial stone is in the corner of the churchyard across the road.

The inn dates back to the mid 1700s and must have served the old packhorse route from Delph to Marsden. As with many rural pubs in the 1990s it has survived through serving good food, and thankfully for the thirsty rambler a wide selection of real brews. The inn retains a certain charm lost in places that have been refurbished in the modern pub idiom. There are all sorts of interesting things to look at, besides the handpumps, including the mounted head of the Peniston Pack, who was killed on the railway line at Wellhouse Cutting in 1896. Not quite everyone's cup of tea but interesting nevertheless.

Unfortunately, the inn is not open weekday lunchtimes except for pre-booked parties. Nevertheless, The Royal Oak is a rugged survivor amidst good moorland walking and is not too far from the Pennine Way should you decide on a more energetic trek.

Castleshaw

Join the tarmac road and turn right. At the cross roads, it is possible to go ahead but, instead of following the track towards the farm, cut diagonally right across the field on your right to the far corner where the track is joined again by way of a gap stile. Go right along the track as it descends. There are views across to Castleshaw hill and beneath to the reservoirs of the same name. The former is said to be the site of Castleshaw Roman fort dating from approximately 80 AD, a defensive site near to the old Roman road between York and Manchester.

Another track cuts off right but avoid this. Shortly afterwards, go through a stone gateway and follow the broken down wall on the right down the hill a short distance and then go slightly left through hummocky ground. The way is not particularly clear down this hillside but soon there is a metal stile over a wall to cross and continue to head for the storage area by the reservoir hidden by trees and fencing.

While the O.S. Pathfinder map shows a number of paths converging on the storage area, including yours, this has not been the case for some time as the fencing suggests. Follow the perimeter fence around to the right to join a track. Go right and walk down to the footbridge beneath the dam. Do not cross it but keep ahead to another stile and then cross the next footbridge.

Mill Pond

This is a well-walked path back to Delph and the way parallels the banks of the feeder stream. Closer to Delph it comes alongside an old mill pond and to the end of a track by houses. Keep ahead here to follow the stream once again which should now be on your right. This exits by another pool and restored buildings where it cuts left to a road. Go right into the village. In the latter part of the eighteenth century there were several mills along the stream and some of the old ponds feeding them are still discernible, particularly as you approach Delph.

Most pubs in Delph welcome walkers but one which might interest you is The Rose and Crown as it usually has a guest beer on offer as well as Websters bitter. When the authors last called a fine pint of Robinwoods was being served.

The Rose and Crown

10. RAPES HIGHWAY AND STANDEDGE

A classic Pennine walk utilising a medieval packhorse way, a dramatic section of the Pennine Way and an early turnpike road.

Pub: The Railway Inn, Marsden. Tetley Bitter and Mild, Marston's Pedigree. Open Monday to Friday 1200 – 1500 and 1730 – 2300; Sat 1130 – 1600 and 1900-2300; Sun 1200 – 1500 and 1930-2230. No food.

Start: Marsden station

Distance: 6 miles (10 km)

Maps: Pathfinder Sheet 702 Huddersfield and Marsden; Landranger 110 Sheffield and Huddersfield area.

Public transport: Hourly service (Metro Train) on the Huddersfield Line from Leeds/Wakefield/Huddersfield/Stalybridge/Manchester (Victoria) (BR Table 39A); more limited (but adequate) service on Sundays. Yorkshire Rider bus 350/1 from Huddersfield, limited service 365 from Oldham. Metro Day Rover valid.

By Car: Ample car parking in Marsden around the church.

Marsden lies at the top end of the Colne Valley, in a vast green cul-de-sac between the hills. It's a sturdy little West Riding textile town of mills, stone terraces and old, ancient farms surrounded by countryside of bleak grandeur, including the northern edge of the Peak National Park. There is no way west out of the town except by steep hills, creating transport problems which have required remarkable engineering achievements to solve. Little wonder they say Marsden was the last place in Yorkshire to discover the wheel!

The Railway Inn, opposite Marsden Station, makes an ideal start or finishing point for the ramble for this spectacular walk along the summit ridge of the Pennines. The Railway is a typical, unpretentious Pennine

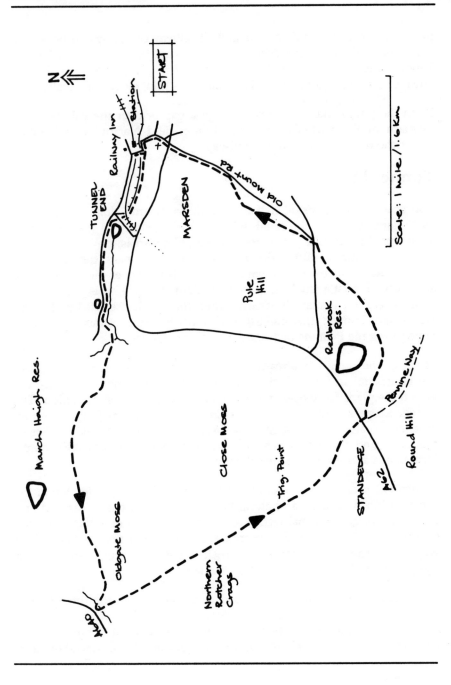

pub almost certainly built by the LNWR railway company and now with a suitable railway theme decor, a roaring coal fire in winter, excellent Tetley's and Marston's on draught, and a friendly atmosphere. There's always something going on at The Railway – mini events and festivals!

From the pub, make your way through a gap or over the stile onto the towpath of the partially restored Huddersfield Narrow Canal, going under the road bridge from the railway.

Tunnel End

You now have a pleasant half mile walk westwards along the towpath by the still waters of the canal, with banks of heather on the old tunnel spoil tips. You pass a picnic area in old siding areas, now wooded, on the left. Continue under the railway lines and pass the handsome Huddersfield Narrow Canal warehouse to a bridge over the canal. Cross, and turn left past a small car park near Tunnel End. This is a fascinating area where the canal disappears into the blackness of the famous Standedge Tunnel, the highest and longest canal tunnel in Britain, penetrating the Pennine bedrock for over three miles.

Much of the canal has already been restored thanks to the initiative of the Huddersfield Canal Society and several local authorities. There are ambitious plans to re-open the tunnel as a major tourist attraction. The former keepers' cottages at Tunnel End have been transformed into an excellent Visitor Centre, open most days of the year, with exhibitions of the canal and the area's rich heritage of transport history, also maps, local books and guides and excellent coffee.

Return to the small car park and walk back up the lane, going left at the Junction Inn (Websters) and along Waters Road. You pass a disused and partially overgrown canal feeder reservoir and a row of cottages to Hey Green where, below the hotel entrance, there is a junction of lanes. Your way is directly ahead for a few metres before bearing left along a signposted path through a metal pedestrian gate.

This leads along an attractive raised causeway above the infant River Colne, eventually emerging at Eastergate Bridge. This narrow, beautifully arched packhorse bridge carried the ancient Trans-Pennine packhorseway, Rapes Highway, on its journey from Rochdale and

Milnrow in Lancashire across to the Colne Valley of Yorkshire. At this point, on the left hand side of the two streams that meet, there was a packhorse inn. This was kept, in the 18th century, by one Esther Schofield whose name was corrupted to 'Easter', the word 'gate' being dialect for road, now applied to the bridge, though the name Close Gate is also sometimes used.

Willykay Clough

The path follows the branching stream to the right for a few metres, before veering up a steep side valley to the left. Follow the signposts, as the path climbs steadily up the ravine. Look for further well-sited wooded signposts as the path bears right once you reach the crest of the hill, dipping down into Willykay Clough, a narrow beck, before heading due westwards. Your clear route is along a narrow path over rough moorgrass, now marked by series of stone posts inscribed PH Road, erected by the local council after a legal dispute early this century. Evidence at this court case came from people who had used the route in their childhood, including an eighty-year old shepherd from Oldham, Sam Garside. He remembered leading his drunken father over the road at eleven o'clock at night, coming back from Marsden Fair, with two hens in a basket and a tup (ram) following on behind.

There are magnificent views on all sides across Oldgate Moor, (its name from the old road) looking back down the Colne Valley or ahead up towards the hill known as March Haigh with its reservoir. After about a mile, you will find yourself curving above and eventually down a shallow ravine, before swinging right to reach the A640 road to meet the Pennine Way at Haigh Gutter, crossed by a footbridge.

Go sharp left now, back across the beck and along the Pennine Way. This is well defined, eroded and boggy in paces, as you bear slightly right to ascend Oldgate Moss towards Northern Rotcher Crags. As the route levels out you enjoy a fine, well-drained sandy path along the edge of the moor with truly magnificent views westwards across the industrial Lancashire plain, with still a few tall chimneys and big square brick mills to give a Lowryesque atmosphere.

Ammon Wrigley

You reach the memorial cairn to Lancashire poet and topographer Ammon Wrigley (1861-1846) who wrote memorably about nearby Saddleworth area. Pass the OS trig point before dropping down to the main A62 in the deep Standedge cutting.

Cross the road, taking care with traffic, turn left and up the road on the sidewalk for a short distance following the Pennine Way signs. Turn right over the stile with the Pennine Way leading onto Rouhe Hill. Where the Pennine Way swings away southwards, bear left behind Redbrook Reservoir along a narrow path over open moor. The path swings northwestwards, crossing becks to join the lane to Marsden at a cross roads.

Cross the road, taking the left fork, Old Mount Road, part of one of the earliest eighteenth century turnpike roads built by Jack Metcalfe, 'Blind Jack o' Knaresborough', the great road engineer, over Standedge for coaches. This was well before the present A62 route was built in the 1820s. Where a green track forks left again, take it, above field enclosures but parallel to the road, descending towards the rooftops of Marsden along the side of Pule Hill.

There is a choice of ways back into Marsden, but the paths get a bit complex to trace. The easiest way is to follow the first fork you reach in the track to the right which brings you back into Old Mount Road by cottages. Walk down into the centre of town, crossing the main A62 and keep straight ahead for Marsden Church.

Enoch Taylor

In the old graveyard, now partially landscaped in the grassed area to your right, there are the old stocks, last used in 1821 and the gravestone of one Enoch Taylor, local blacksmith and maker of shearing frames from 1812 onwards. Taylor's frames were smashed by the Colne valley Luddites who resisted the mechanisation of the wool industry using large hammers. These were also given the name 'Enochs', leading to the famous Luddite saying: 'Enoch makes them and Enoch breaks them.'

Turn left at the church along the riverside and cross at another lovely old packhorse bridge, Mellor Bridge, built in 1772. Go through a narrow enclosed way ahead to the right by a former mill, to emerge alongside the Railway Inn for, if you've timed it right, that concluding pint and train home.

11. THE COLNE VALLEY

Paved causeways, steep hillsides, mills and canals make this Colne valley ramble a typical Pennine experience – with superb local ale at the celebrated Sair Inn.

Pub: The Sair Inn, Linthwaite. Linfit Mild, Special Bitter, Leadboiler, Old Eli and Enoch's Hammer, English Guineas Stout and Xmas ale. Open Monday to Friday 1900 -2300 (closed lunchtimes); Saturday 1100 – 1500 and 1900 – 2300; Sunday 1200 – 1500 and 1900 – 2230. No food.

Start: Slaithwaite village centre

Distance: 4 miles (6 km)

Map: Pathfinder Sheet 702 Huddersfield and Marsden; Landranger Sheet 110 Sheffield and Huddersfield.

Public Transport: Hourly Metro Train service (Sundays two hourly) Huddersfield Line (Leeds/Wakefield – Huddersfield- Manchester BR Table 39A). Choice of Yorkshire Rider buses from Huddersfield, including buses to Marsden along Manchester Road and the Colne Valley circular (362). Metro Day Rover valid in West Yorkshire.

By Car: Park in centre of Slaithwaite in car park opposite Globe Mill.

Slaithwaite, correctly pronounced "Slathwaite" or even "Slawit", is a typical Colne valley mill town in the steep sided Colne Valley, the hillsides compressing river, railway, canal and mill communities into mainly linear settlements. Slaithwaite, like others in the Colne Valley owes its existence to availability of water power, provided not only by the River Colne but by three fast flowing Pennine tributary streams. Industry grew with the opening of the Huddersfield Narrow Canal in 1798 through the valley which brought in raw materials and exported finished cloth.

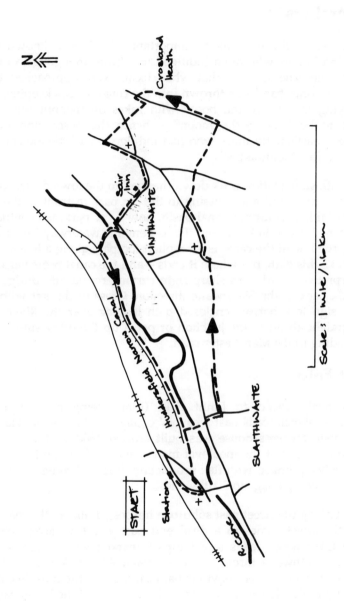

Moonrakers

For a time, Slaithwaite was an important inland port, known for its unruly inhabitants who often indulged in a little smuggling to increase their income. The story is that when locals were approached by the excisemen, contraband was thrown into the canal for safekeeping. When seen trying to retrieve the booty with rakes on moonlit nights they claimed to be "raking the moon" – hence the description of local characters, particularly those who had indulged in a little too much ale, as Slaithwaite "Moonrakers".

From Slaithwaite Station walk down the road to the town centre, turning left at the cross road and crossing to the car park in front of the Globe Worsted Mill. This former canal basin, now a car park, is eventually to be reopened as a link in this Trans-Pennine waterway. At time of writing, the line of the canal is an asphalt footpath along a linear area of grass. Take this path, but where it ends – and the canal begins again – at an interpretive board, turn sharp right curving round into Bridge Street and walk back in the Slaithwaite direction. Cross to the left with a 'no cycling' sign to a narrow enclosed path leading over the River Colne. Keep straight ahead at the junction of paths up the other side to stone steps leading to the Manchester road.

Linfit Fold

Cross directly ahead to Linfit Fold (Linfit being a corruption of Linthwaite), which leads past weavers' cottages to Linthwaite Hall. This fine yeoman farmer's house was built around 1600 by the Lockwood family on the site of the medieval manor house of the de Lynthwaites, the name being linked with flax production. It is said to be haunted and to have a secret passage to Slaithwaite.

Turn left along the street past suburban houses parallel to the main road. Where the street comes to a dead end past a traffic barrier, continue along a track which leads to a footpath marked with a sign to Ston's Lane and Linthwaite through a stile ahead. At a fork bear right to a stone gap stile and a very obvious path carved into the hillside climbing diagonally to the right to another stile in the brow of the hill ahead. This then contours round the hillside to another stile, before descending towards Linthwaite straight ahead, past the ends of suburban street and laurel bushes to become an enclosed way by gardens. Turn left in the lane into Linthwaite.

At the Methodist Chapel fork right into Chapel Hill which soon climbs uphill and becomes Wain Hill, past a new Jehovah's Witness meeting house. At the next cross roads look for the path right immediately behind the telephone kiosk and letterbox which is a flagged path between house gardens. Follow this uphill to a road by a bus stop where, almost directly opposite, the path continues through a low stone gap stile. A straight paved way climbs up the hillside between the playing fields of Colne Valley High School.

The path meets a narrow lane. Turn left and follow the lane along the brow of the hill with fine views below you across the Colne Valley. After about 300 metres, opposite the blue panelled classrooms of Colne Valley School below, look for a narrow stony path on the right going between the heather and young pine trees onto Crossland Heath. Follow this path uphill to where it meets another path along the moor edge. Walk through the heather, with superb moorland views.

Slaid

This path soon begins to descend and rejoins the lane just above and to the east of a group of cottages known as Slaid. Turn left here, back to the cottages where, on the right, past the tall three-storey block of weavers' cottages on the right you'll see a path marked by a tall concrete lamp post above some steps.

Take this as it leads to another paved path – this time over an open field before becoming enclosed between walls by cottages to join a lane. Cross this, continuing directly opposite, again on a flagged path between a wall and an old railway sleeper fence to emerge on the road at Broad Oak by a farm. Turn left into the road and continue past the church and road junction, and just before the petrol filling station turn sharp right down Tommy Lane, a steep and narrow lane past cottages and houses. At the junction turn right again to the Sair Inn in the lane.

The Sair Inn is a mecca for real ale enthusiasts, with its own choice Linfit brewery ales and a cosy wood fire in winter. There is a remarkable collection of bottles around the walls, a replica of Enoch's Hammer (see Walk 10) and lots of No Poll Tax and similar notices in the radical Colne Valley tradition.

It used to be a home brewery over a hundred years ago when it first acquired the nick-name 'Sair' after the locals found the beer to be sour on one occasion. Eli Dyson, the then brewer cum publican did not take too kindly to the name but it stuck! Once again, home brewed ales are on offer – and what a range to choose from, including a popular stout.

From the Sair Inn, continue downhill to the Manchester road at Hoy Fold. Cross and turn left, but after a few metres go right down steps into Lowestwood Lane. Continue across the River Colne to the towpath of the Huddersfield New Canal. Turn left along the recently restored towpath.

It is easy walking now through a classic Pennine mill-and-canal landscape, past several massive mills with their millponds, the canal threading its way forward through the valley to Slaithwaite. Just before you reach the town you reach the canal basin blockage and rejoin the footpath on the canal bed to the centre of Slaithwaite. If you are going back by train and have time to kill before your train, both the Commercial Hotel and the Shoulder of Mutton Inn supply a very acceptable pint of Stones and draught Bass, Bitter and Mild.

12. LITTLEBOROUGH

The "Weighver's Seaport" has been a place of recreation in the Pennines for well over one hundred years. This is a gentle ramble from Littleborough to and around Hollingworth Lake returning along the Rochdale Canal.

Pub: The Queen's, Church Street, Littleborough. Thwaites Mild and Bitter. Open Monday, Wednesday, Thursday 1200 – 1500 and 1800 – 2300; Tuesdays not open at lunchtimes, only 1800 – 2300 hours; Fridays 1200 – 2300; Saturday 1200 – 1500 and 1900 – 2300; Sunday 1200 – 1500 and 1900 – 2230. Bar snacks available until 8 pm.

Start: Littleborough Railway Station

Distance: 6 miles (10 km)

Map: Ordnance Survey South Pennines Leisure Sheet No 21

Public Transport: Littleborough railway station enjoys a daily service from Manchester and Leeds. The town is also well served by local buses including one which calls at Hollingworth Lake, thus allowing a cut off point on the ramble.

By Car: Travel on the A58 from Rochdale or Halifax. There is car parking near The Coach House in Littleborough.

Littleborough grew as a settlement near to the banks of the River Roth, a valley which became increasingly important as transport links were built and mills took the place of weaver homesteads in the hillsides. With this rapid industrial growth came chapels and churches, pubs, corner shops and trams. Standing in the square by the station, it is not difficult to imagine what life would have been like in this bustling centre during the latter part of the last century.

The old Coach House is now a heritage centre and the local community has done an excellent job in interpreting the industrial and social history of the locality. Throughout the town you will also find little plaques

providing useful snippets of historical information about many of the
local buildings including the pubs.

One such inn is the Queen's in Church street, a lovely little Thwaites
pub dating from the last century. The lintel above the door suggests
1861. A local pub historian, however, considers that it might not have
become a pub until 1872 as this is the first recorded date of a licensee.
The pub, recommended in CAMRA's Good Beer Guide, offers a warm
welcome and has recently been refurbished in Victorian style. The rich
dark mild beer is exceptionally good, so try a drop before or after the
walk.

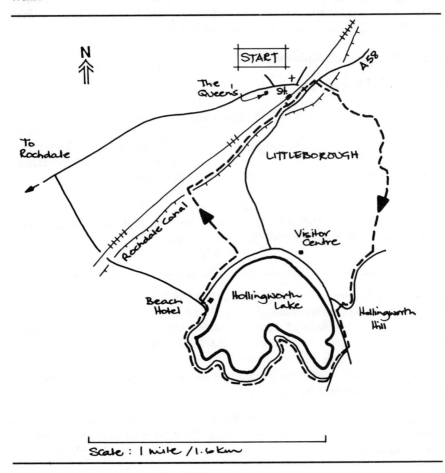

From the booking office go left under the subway and follow the road around to the left passing by the garage. Another road joins from beneath the railway and you keep right to pass The Red Lion and then go right up Ealees Road to cross over the canal. Pass by old cottages, allotments, and mills, following the track signposted to Hollingworth.

Whittaker

The track eventually begins to curve sharp left. At this point, go over the bridge, then take the higher track, rather than the well-worn path to the Visitor Centre, following the fence and then the wall. As this green lane curves left, go ahead to cross a stile, with the old settlement of Whittaker above to your left. Keep company with the wall on your left to cross another stile and proceed ahead through wet and rough ground. Cut the corner and head for a tree. Walk over the bridge and head slightly left to the field corner to go through a gateway snd then turn right.

Go right through another stile by an electric telegraph pole and then walk up the bank to a meet another well worn path by the perimeter fence. Bear right to follow the feeder channel up to a gate and then to exit ahead by a cottage onto a lane at Hollingworth Fold, a very old settlement on the road to Ogden.

Hollingworth Lake

Turn right with views to your left up to Rakewood and the M62. As the road curves, cut left down a path to another road by the side of the lake. Turn left (unless making a detour right to the Visitor Centre) and then go next right and right again. As this road curves left, keep ahead to follow the lakeside around to an exit by The Beach Hotel, which has a pleasant garden overlooking the lake and offers draught beer. This is one of the few survivors for during the last century, when Hollingworth was a very popular local resort, there were several pubs and hotels to cater for the needs of the visitor. The nick-name "Weighver's Seaport" came about because so many visitors were escaping the mills of the North West to take a breath of fresh air at Hollingworth. Swimming, boating and fishing and strolling were the main pastimes. Swimming became particularly popular after the famous Captain Webb, the man who swam the English Channel in 1875, tried a few lengths across the lake.

The lake lost its popularity as a resort with the advent of mass travel by car, but can still get uncomfortably busy on warm Sunday afternoons. The country park and visitor centre offer opportunities to learn about the locality, as well as being ideal for picnics. When built in the late eighteenth century to serve the needs of industrialists and canal engineers, the sponsors would not have guessed that it would be such an attraction for the visitor two centuries later.

Rochdale Canal

On the road turn right and at the end of the houses go left down Heald Lane. The path leads ahead through the farmyard which gets into a terrible state after wet weather. Keep ahead down the hill by the works along a green track to cross the Rochdale Canal, a stretch of navigation between Sowerby Bridge and Rochdale. Begun in 1794, it took well nearly ten years to complete.

Turn right to join the towpath and walk back for a mile alongside The Rochdale Canal to Littleborough returning to the main road by The Railway public house.

13. RAMSBOTTOM

An exhilarating walk onto the moors dominated by Peel Tower, a monument seen from miles around.

Pub: The Royal Oak, Ramsbottom; Thwaites Mild and Bitter.

Usual Opening Hours: Monday to Friday 1200 – 1700 and 1900 – 2300 hours. Saturdays 1200 – 2300 hours. Sundays 1200 – 1500 and 1900 – 2230 hours.

Distance: 7 miles (11 km).

Map: Pathfinder Sheet 700 Bolton (North) & Horwich. Landranger 109 Manchester.

Public Transport: By rail from Bury on the East Lancs railway; many buses from Manchester and Bury. Up to the minute timetable information can be obtained by 'phoning 061 228 7811.

By Car: Ramsbottom is signed from the M66 or A56 from Bury. There is car parking by the railway station.

The Royal Oak, in Bridge Street, Ramsbottom has been a firm favourite with CAMRA for some years and features regularly in both local and national Good Beer Guides. This three roomed pub with a smaller snug lounge, a main lounge and a games room is served by a well located bar with handpull Thwaites's mild and bitter offered in superb condition. It is a friendly pub which appeals to locals but there is always a welcome for visitors.

Ramsbottom

Ramsbottom is very much a Lancashire mill town of the Rossendale valley where textile production reigned supreme along the banks of the Irwell. The area was also known for the ancillary processes of bleaching and dyeing and to a lesser extent for quarrying of stone and mining of coal. Early historians have chronicled the poor working and living

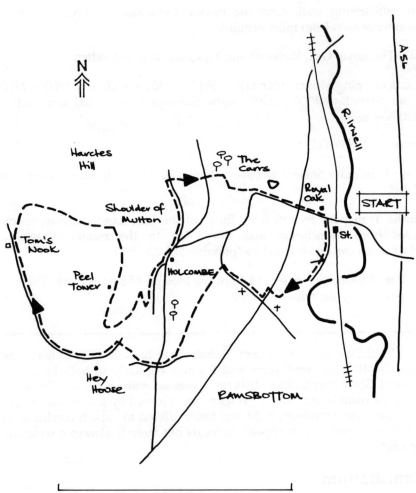

N

Harcles Hill

The Carrs

R. Irwell

A56

Royal Oak

START

Shoulder of Mutton

St.

Tom's Nook

HOLCOMBE

Peel Tower

Hey House

RAMSBOTTOM

Scale : 1 mile / 1.6 km

conditions of the workforce including their drinking habits. Many of the mill owners were concerned to stamp out the latter as much on economic as moral grounds. One such family was the Grants, merchants from Manchester who moved into the area to extend their textile ownership. As their economic power grew so did their interest in the town's infrastructure. They sponsored roads, churches and other town institutions, many of which survive today. There's a good street market in the town on one Sunday per month.

Start from Ramsbottom railway station. This station is home to the East Lancs railway and is operated now as a leisure railway offering both diesel and steam-hauled trains at weekends. The main terminus and museum is at Bury and the restoration work along the line has been tremendous in the past five years, including Ramsbottom station itself.

Cobden Mill

At the corner, keep ahead with Cobden mill, now in a sorry state across the road to your right and a major distribution company on your left. Follow this narrower road to the next corner and go right and then within a few paces left along a paved path leading up towards the church. This reaches the main road where you cross the road, turn left and then turn next right by the pub. Walk past some interesting gardens for they are divided by stone slab walls. Note the old chapel on the opposite side of the road at the junction of school street.

Peel Monument

There are views from here of Holcombe church and also Peel Monument. The latter is 112 to 120 feet high (depending on which source you read!) and built of gritstone quarried from the moor surrounding it in 1852. It was ceremoniously opened by Frederick Peel, a younger son of Robert Peel who became the Prime Minister responsible for reforming the Corn Laws and introducing a Metropolitan police force (the 'peelers' or 'bobbies'). The tower was built to commemorate the repeal of the Corn Laws which reduced the heavy duty on corn and hence made the staple diet of bread more affordable to working people. As with many of these follies, it was paid for by local public subscription and has recently been restored to weather another hundred years on the moors.

Walk a short distance farther before turning left, before the corner, into Downfield Close. Go up the steps between houses, turn left and then exit right into a field which comes as a pleasant relief from road walking. Go straight ahead along a well worn path but keep above the tree line and then diverging slightly right a small wood, across a clough and cross a stile. The path comes to a junction but keep ahead to cross another dip and then go through the stone gap stile. Proceed across the field on the clear path which curves left as it nears the houses and exit by way of a steep stone stile onto the lane. Turn right here and walk up to the main road.

Go over the road and walk up to the junction and entrance to an Islamic College. Take the road just to your right, marked private, by the old gate-house and, shortly, as the lane curves left, turn right. Within a few paces go left to cross a stile and walk up the field between fences to another lane. Go left and follow this lane ahead, passing at first a complex of buildings at Hey House and then passing a farm. The track becomes rougher and rises past the scant remains of former farms and barns, now part of a training ground for the army. The views up the Holcombe valley and up to Holcombe Moor become more impressive as you gain ground.

Tom's Nook

The track begins to descend for a short while and bends left to pass by a more substantial ruin, known as Tom's Nook. Go right here up a wet narrow track thick with sedge grass. This climbs to a stream but do not cross it. Turn right to join the level moor, with Haracles hill ahead and a gentle gap just to the right of it. There is a small pile of stones as a marker point within thirty paces and a narrow path resembling a sheep walk heading slightly right of the gap. Follow this, passing by four small concrete posts. In a short distance, this path meets a main path coming down from Haracles hill to Peel Monument. Turn right onto it and walk to the tower.

Holcombe

There are two paths down. You can either turn left and cut down right after a short distance or follow the track from the tower on the right which curves sharp left before the house and then progresses down the hillside to join another lane. Turn left and follow Cross Lane into Holcombe village. Across the road is The Shoulder of Mutton, an unusual pub in that it serves Vaux's draught beers, an independent brewery based in Sunderland of all places. The pub car park is also the bus turning point so it is possible to return to Bury from here. Holcombe is one of the least changed villages in the area lying on the old packhorse route from Bury to Haslingden. Most of the houses date from the seventeenth or eighteenth century and reflect life before the industrial growth of the Rossendale valley when agriculture and homestead weaving dominated rather than mills.

Just beyond the pub is a turn left, signed as a bridleway, which leads away from the village towards the moor again. You come to a junction and at this point turn right, through a stile and down a steep walled lane to a main road. Cross over and continue down the hill but cross a stile shortly on your left. The path dips down to the stream in this wooded area known locally as The Carrs. The path curves right before reaching the stream and follows through an old stile. It then curves right and exits onto a road by two large shrubs.

Some locals use the road but the path is signed right and left to pass the perimeter of a house and garden. It then drops back down onto the road where you turn right. Pass by the Rose and Crown and walk down the street into the centre of Ramsbottom, noticing no doubt the pool on the left and lower down Ramsbottom's heritage centre. At the crossroads keep ahead into Bridge Street and follow this down to pass Bailey's Tea Shop and then The Royal Oak. A little farther along, cross the road and turn right by The Railway hotel and back to the East Lancashire Railway.

14. RYBURNDALE

Some spectacular countryside along one of the major tributary valleys of the River Calder

Pubs: The Blue Ball, High Soyland, Ripponden: Taylor's Bitter, Landlord, Gold Best and Dark Mild; Theakstones Bitter; John Smith's Bitter. Open Monday to Saturday 1100 – 1500 (except Tuesday lunchtimes) and 1900 – 2300; Sunday 1200 – 1500 and 1900 – 2230. Food daily 1200 – 1400 and 1900 – 2200.

Old Bridge Inn, Ripponden: Taylor's Bitter and Golden Best Mild, Youngers Scotch and Webster's Bitter Open Monday to Saturday 1130 – 1530 and 1730 – 2300; Sundays 1200 – 1500 and 1900 – 2230. Food daily 1200 – 1400 and 1900 – 2145

Start: Ripponden

Distance: 6 miles (10 km)

Map: Ordnance Survey Outdoor Leisure Sheet 21 South Pennines.

Public Transport: Metro Train Calderdale Line to Sowerby Bridge Station (BR Table 40) then bus 528, 560 to Ripponden. Through bus 556 from Manchester, Oldham Halifax and 528 from Rochdale. Day Rover valid within West Yorkshire.

By Car: Park in free car park in Royd Lane, Ripponden (on the right 100 metres traffic lights if coming from Halifax direction).

Ripponden is one of those long, narrow Pennine mill towns which seems to be squeezed into a valley around a long line of formerly water powered mills. The Ryburn Valley was particularly famous for the manufacture of hard wearing blue cloth used by the Royal Navy – Navy Blue. It was also at an important cross roads and staging post on ancient Trans-Pennine roads between Halifax, Rochdale and Oldham. Even though the M62 has taken most of its heavy traffic away, it still has the feeling of a town nestling on the edge of wild country and the end of

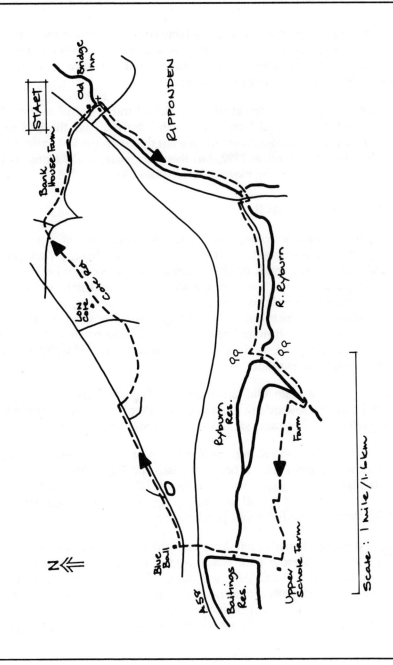

high moorland passes. Its branch railway from Sowerby Bridge closed in
1929, but frequent Yorkshire Rider buses from the bottom of the main
entrance road to Sowerby Bridge Station make it easy to reach from
West Yorkshire or Greater Manchester.

From Royd Lane bus stop (at Sowerby side of traffic lights) in the village
centre, take the cobbled lane towards the church. Pass the Old Bridge
Inn (no inn sign, but don't assume it's not open) on the left, cross the old
packhorse bridge, built in 1722, but then turn sharp right along cobbled
Mill Fold underneath the more modern Elland Road bridge.

Weavers Cottages

This passes weavers' cottages and leads to a children's playground and
new park by the riverside. You can walk through here, picking up the
continuation of the track by the riverside, past a weir and a small new
business park. Keep to the riverside where the main tracks swings away
left, the path going through riverside woodland, rising to an embankment past mills which are still working, producing plastics rather than
textiles. Ignore a footbridge but continue until you reach a broad bridge
leading to a mill yard, Whiteley's Mill, where at time of writing, Code 3
Safety Equipment is made.

Walk up to the main Oldham road, crossing carefully. Turn right for
about 20 metres towards the bus stop and shop in the curve of the road,
going left along Bar Lane, signposted to Ryburn Paper Mill.

Follow this quiet lane along the Ryburn, past cottages and an old mill
dam, now a Trout Farm. When you reach the Paper Mill, once famous
for its high quality paper used for Bibles, take the track under the tall
archway between the mill buildings, signposted as a footpath. This
climbs steadily above the mill pond behind the mill.

Where the track hairpins left, keep straight ahead to the left of a double
garage along a narrow path which leads to a stile and steps to ascend
Ryburn Reservoir Dam. Turn left along the dam, then right along a
beautiful wooded path alongside the water's edge. Curve round to the
head of the southern arm of the reservoir where there is a footbridge
across the feeder beck, and a path signed to New Barn and Heights.

Cross the bridge, climbing through the woods along another enclosed path to a stile at the top of the wood. The path continues alongside the wall, up steps, with the wall on your right. This leads to a pedestrian gate and into another enclosed path between walls to a farm. The path goes through a ramshackle gate immediately to the right of the farm buildings, leading to a path enclosed between the wall and a wire fence. Keep ahead to the next stile, and alongside the wall on the right, the path slowly ascending until you join an ancient enclosed green track at a gap.

Turn right here, but as the track bends left take the stile right and cross to ruined buildings with a footpath sign. There are impressive views across the Upper Ryburn valley from here, its characteristic mixture of scattered farms, small enclosures, reservoirs and moorland.

High Wormald

Keep left at the buildings as directed by the sign to join another green track leading to another farm ahead, High Wormald. Go through the gate into the farmyard and just past the farm, go through the field gate on the right (waymarked) and follow a field track diagonally across to the next farm, Upper Schole Carr, and into its farmyard.

Immediately past this farm, turn sharp right into the enclosed track between wire fences which dips down to a gate and the track across the top of Baitings Reservoir Dam, emerging at a small car park (with loos) on the A58 Blackstone Edge road. Take the grassy path alongside the wall on the right which climbs from the New Inn car park to the Blue Ball Inn, whose low white buildings will have been a landmark for some time.

This lovely old Timothy Taylor's pub has a justifiably fine reputation for its beer. It's an old packhorseman's pub, rich in atmosphere and reputedly haunted, and existed before the present "new" turnpike road over Blackstone Edge. A good range of food is on offer at lunchtime and evenings, and there is an attractive sun lounge with fine views. Note the Blue Ball rhyme over the door.

From the Blue Ball turn left along Blue Ball Road, a quiet moorland road which may have originally been a Roman Road, above and parallel to the valley, ignoring roads forking off right and left. Pass above a small reservoir for about half a mile, and the junction with Ripponden Old Lane, then take the next unsurfaced track to the right, London Spring Road. This passes London Spring Farm and becomes a sandy way through heather again contouring around the hillside along the edge of a low ridge, the views now to the left. At the cross roads, go straight ahead along the unsurfaced track almost opposite, Cote Road. This soon passes a superb, if neglected, 17th century farmhouse, Low Cote, the word "cote" being old English for cottage or farmhouse. This track emerges at yet another cross roads.

Keep ahead on the track which curves down to another cross roads, again going ahead, past a farm, Bank House Head. This time, where the more obvious track swings left, take a much narrower footpath, not immediately obvious, straight ahead behind the farm, soon descending to become a lovely enclosed way between stone walls.

Where it meets a junction of tracks, turn right to the lane, and go left steeply downhill into the outskirts of Ripponden. Bear right into what is now Royd Lane to the car park and bus stop where you might well use any available time before a bus at the remarkable Old Bridge Inn.

This is believed to be the oldest pub in Yorkshire, dating from 1313 and before that time having probably been a Guest House of a small monastery on what were important Trans-Pennine bridle roads. Daniel Defoe is reputed to have stayed here on his celebrated Journey Through England in the 1720s, and also King Christian of Denmark. The building is of medieval cruck construction with much fine detail in the interior, including early stooth panelling, an ancient stone fireplace and deeply worn stonework. It also sells extremely good beer and there is food available both in the pub and the restaurant "Under the Bridge" just across the river, open in the evenings.

15. HEATH COMMON

A walk of startling contrast in the gentler foothills of the eastern Pennines, travelling from heavy industry to totally unspoiled 18th century rural England in barely a mile.

Pub: The King's Arms, Heath. Clark's Bitter and King's Mild, Taylor's Landlord. Open Monday to Friday 1130 – 1500 and 1800 – 2300; Saturday 1130 – 2300; Sunday 1200 – 1500 and 1900 – 2230. Food daily 1200 – 1400.

Start: Wakefield Kirkgate Station

Distance: 5 miles (8 km)

Map: Pathfinder Sheet 692 (703 not essential); Landranger 104, 111

Public Transport: Hourly (Sundays, two hourly) service (Metro Train) on the Hallam Line (Leeds-Wakefield-Barnsley-Sheffield line – BR table 34; Metro Train Huddersfield line hourly (Sundays restricted) from Huddersfield with connection from Manchester – BR Table 39A). Kirkgate is 10 minutes' walk from Westgate (InterCity) station. Metro Day Rover ticket valid.

By Car: Park in Wakefield (choice of well signed car parks) and join walk at Kirkgate Station.

Wakefield, the oldest town in West Yorkshire and until recently, the county town of both the West Riding and recently abolished West Yorkshire County Councils, was a Saxon settlement. It evolved as an important Saxon trading settlement at the then navigable limit of the River Calder and bridging point. It also saw action in the Wars of the Roses when, in 1460, a huge Lancastrian army commanded by Lord Clifford defeated the Duke of York. By the Industrial Revolution its waterway and railway communications helped it become a major centre for textiles, engineering and coal mining, a position which it still maintains.

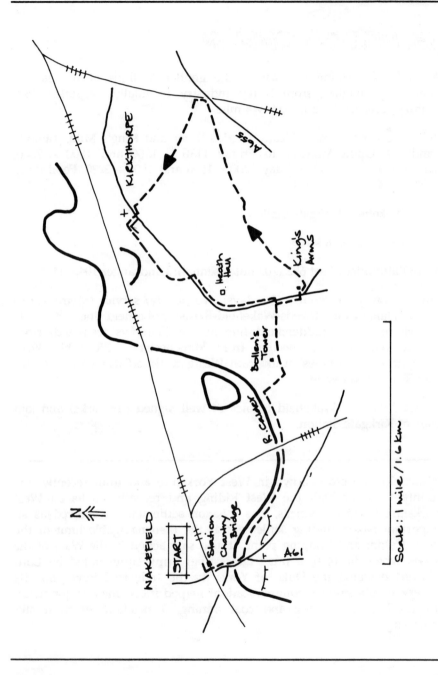

Kirkgate

Kirkgate Station is an appropriate starting point for this walk of contrasts. If its interior, long since roofless, is but a ghost of its former self, its exterior remains grand and unspoiled. This handsome early Victorian neo-classical building of 1857 once lay on the first Trans-Pennine railway line, the Manchester and Leeds Railway, through the Calder Valley, later to become the important Lancashire and Yorkshire Railway. Note the L&Y insignia and the handsome clock; all that is missing are the crinolines and carriages of the once-busy Victorian railway metropolis when, as long ago as 1888, crack L&Y steam expresses could get from Manchester (Victoria), 47 miles away, to Wakefield in a mere 58 minutes, somewhat faster than today's Sprinters.

From the station entrance, turn sharp left by the Wakefield Arms (a pleasant Tetley's pub) down a stone flagged, enclosed path to the main road beneath the railway. Turn left and continue past the cash-and-carry warehouses and toilets, following the pedestrian-sign to Chantry Bridge.

Chantry

This lovely medieval stone bridge, now mercifully by-passed by the roaring Doncaster road traffic, carries one of only four surviving bridge Chantries in England, dating from the mid 14th century, in Decorated style though heavily restored last century. Dedicated to St. Mary, it is still used for the occasional service and is normally closed to the public.

At the far side of the bridge take a gap to a narrow packhorse bridge on the left which leads to a pleasant area of grass alongside river and bridge. There is a not very obvious path here, going parallel to the River Calder and alongside a tall galvanised fence. Keep ahead past the fence, as the strip of land narrows, to reach a metal footbridge which crosses the canalised arm of the Aire and Calder Navigation as it locks away from the river to the right. There is usually a commercial barge or river tug moored nearby.

Keep ahead in the same direction alongside the navigable River Calder, soon going under a bridge carrying a mineral railway. Continue alongside the perimeter fence of a power station, its cooling towers like gigantic sculptures with an impressive beauty of their own.

Follow the path around the perimeter fence to the right, away from the river and soon joining the power station drive. Go left here, but turn right again just past a sub-station along an enclosed way, still alongside the perimeter fence, but by now through an attractive grove of trees.

Bollen's Water Tower

On the left is a curious stone, square tower. This is Dame Mary Bollen's Water Tower, a remarkable structure built in 1650 to provide water for her home at nearby Heath Old Hall, and powered by a waterwheel pump. A 19th century wheel survives. A narrow gap in the fence gives access to the building – see photograph at the end of this walk.

Turn left at the junction of paths, the way now gradually ascending between open fields (fine views of the Pennines behind) to emerge at an iron fieldgate in the outskirts of Heath. Walk on in the same direction across the edge of the Common until you meet a tarmac lane.

Heath

Heath is an astonishing unspoiled, almost entirely 18th century country village, so very close to Wakefield's city centre. Its grand country houses and cottages are set in the lovely open expanse of Heath Common, a village green on a quite extraordinary scale.

As well as the Elizabethan Old Hall itself, there is Heath House, soon visible ahead, designed by the remarkable 18th century architect James Paine. Just to the left is Heath Hall, a masterpiece by his contemporary John Carr of York (designer of Harewood House) with Dower House, another fine dwelling, nearby.

Turn right along the tarmac road to a group of cottages, among them the King's Arms, a remarkably unspoiled 18th century tavern overlooking the expanse of the Common.

This unique country inn with its stone floors, tiny snug, gas lights, antique furnishings, serves the most superb Clark's beer, bitter and mild, brewed little over a mile away in Wakefield. Excellent food is also on offer, and for anyone who decides that is enough for the day, there is even a regular West Riding bus back into Wakefield (service 192).

Otherwise turn left outside the pub for 50 metres, going left at the 'no entry' sign along a long tarmac drive across the 'Common leading between the two fine stone Georgian houses ahead. A curved beech hedge is a notable landmark to the left. Now leave the drive to keep directly ahead between the houses. Look for the wooden footpath sign indicating a stile by the house garden leading to a narrow, enclosed footpath between tall beeches hedges.

The path climbs gently, to a kissing gate. Now bear half right across a field to the next kissing gate, and across the field to a stile. The path now turns left along a hedge and wallside through scrubby grass on the fieldside for some 50 metres, before bearing off half right across the field to a stile marked by marker posts in the hedge ahead. Keep the same direction to another marker post at a little footbridge over a ditch. Cross the next field to the railway and road bridge ahead alongside the A655, to a junction of paths with twin metal footpath signs.

Your way is now along the bridleway which at first runs alongside the old railway trackbed, a disused mineral line. You soon bear left alongside a wood and climb gently, with fine views back across the Pennines, with Emley Moor Television Mast (Yorkshire Television) a notable landmark.

The track, a grassy way, crosses the brow of the hill and descends gently, with magnificent views across the city of Wakefield with its Cathedral, down to the village of Kirkthorpe.

Kirkthorpe

Take time to look at this delightful little 15th century Gothic church with its Perpendicular tower. There are some fine 17th and 18th gravestones and an unusual feature is two pinnacles from the original medieval tower relocated by the church door.

Your route is along the track immediately to the left of the church. Follow it round to the left across an attractive cobbled area to a tarmac lane at the gates of Warmfield House. Your path is left into the woods, on a narrow path curving on an embankment with glimpses between the trees across flooded gravel workings. In the valley and the old arm of the River Calder now cut off by the canalised Aire Calder Navigation to the west.

Keep on the main line of path avoiding a branching path to the right, until it curves round left to rejoin the road to Heath, east of Heath House and Hall.

Keep ahead as the road swings left until you reach the Common. You can now make your way across the grass to the far right hand corner of the common where you'll find the metal gate leading to field path which descends to the power station. Keep right around the perimeter fence, back to the riverside, over the footbridge across the Navigation to Chantry Bridge and the centre of Wakefield.

Bollen Tower

16. OAKWELL HALL

A short walk rich in cultural emphasis: an Elizabethan house, an eighteenth century courthouse pub and a seventeenth century home of prosperous Yorkshire mill owners with a strong Brontë association.

Pub: Black Bull Inn, Birstall. Marston's Pedigree, Castle Eden, Traditional Trophy Cask. Open: Saturday, Monday & Tuesday 1130 – 1500; 1900 -2300; Wednesday, Thursday and Friday 1130 – 2300; Sunday 1200 – 1500 and 1900 – 2230. Food daily 1200 – 1400.

Start: Oakwell Hall Country Park Car Park, Bradford Road, Birstall

Distance: 3 miles (5 km)

Map: Pathfinder Sheet 692; Landranger Sheet 104

Public transport: Yorkshire/Yorkshire Rider services 251 or 252 provide frequent links (Sundays included) to Oakwell Hall Country Park's west entrance from Bradford Interchange or Dewsbury Bus Station, the latter being less than five minutes' walk from Dewsbury Rail Station on Metro train Huddersfield Line.

By Car: Park at Oakwell Hall Country Park Car Park, which lies on the main A652 Bradford-Dewsbury road just south of the M62 motorway.

Though this is a short walk, distance is irrelevant compared with the variety of interest along the route, making it an ideal ramble for a wet day or in the heart of winter.

From the entrance to Oakwell Hall take the path to the left of the car park (not the enclosed bridlepath farther to the left), going straight ahead past the car park and picnic areas to the new Visitor Centre, which is well worth a visit (toilets to rear). As an interpretive board by the footpath explains, much of the present Country Park was reclaimed from the workings of Gomersal Colliery which closed in 1973.

The way to Oakwell Hall continues immediately to the left of the Visitor Centre. It is easy to follow, through the pedestrian kissing gate ahead and along the hardcore path across open grassland towards the Hall which will soon appear ahead, the path descending to cross Oakwell Beck at a footbridge, climbing steps to emerge at the lawn of Oakwell Hall. The entrance to the house is directly ahead.

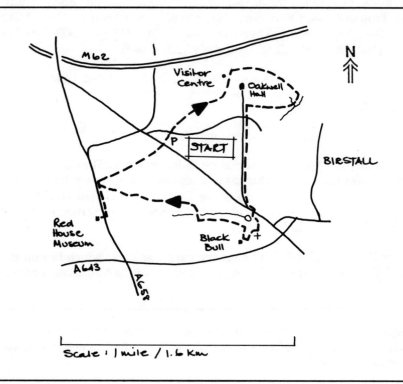

Oakwell Hall

Oakwell Hall is one of the finest surviving small Tudor houses in the North of England. It was probably developed from a fifteenth century timber framed building which was encased in stone and remodelled by its Elizabethan owner, John Batt, whose initials with the date 1583 can still be seen over the door. With only a few minor alterations in the early seventeenth century, the house remains much as it was 350 years ago, with extensive original panelling. It has been superbly furnished in the period of William and Mary (1690) and is open on most days of the year, Sundays from 1300 only.

Outside there is a delightfully reconstructed 17th century herb garden, and close by in restored stabled areas there are craft galleries, an excellent visitor centre and shop and a cafeteria.

Oakwell Hall

Continue the walk by returning to the front of the house and take the path on the left alongside the west side of the house and past the Wildlife garden. Head towards a gap stile into the bridlepath at an old railway bridge. Go through here, crossing the bridlepath with care (galloping horses) but don't cross the bridge, instead keeping right along the path which runs along the top of the railway cutting. This soon heads for a narrow, tall embankment, marked with steps. This is a fine viewpoint across the whole of the country park and the Spen Valley, with the distant mast of Emley Moor television tower (Yorkshire television) a notable landmark to the south. You are close to the roar of the M62 motorway but otherwise this is a delightful oasis of green.

Follow the trail as it descends the embankment, past birch trees, but at a crossroads of paths take the narrow path to the right. This runs parallel with the stream into a shallow valley, past oak and birch woods, soon crossing at a wooden footbridge to enter the woods. Keep on the main path but where you see a stile leading out of the woods ahead. Look for and take a crossing path to the right which drops down to another footbridge over the beck and stiles re-crossing the bridleway. This path ascends a field but keeps inside the next stone fieldwall before bearing left into a grassy picnic area and a stone ramp into the Oakwell Hall car park.

Taylor Fields

Continue left down the main driveway from Oakwell Hall, crossing Nova Lane where, to the left of a large stone building ahead, a track continues along the edge of open fields known as Taylor Fields. Follow this track until it emerges on the main Bradford Road by Peartree Cottage. Cross with care, turning left for about 50 metres to where a path opens on the right leading to and around a pond. Known as Longbottom's Dam, this served Longbottom's dyeworks close by. The old works were only recently demolished.

Go round the pond and cross to Birstall's fine church, with a tower dating from 1100, its top added in 1490 in Perpendicular style, though the rest of the building was rebuilt in the 1860s.

To the right and behind the church lies the Black Bull. This is an excellent example of a village inn built to refresh parishioners who had walked some distance to worship. The present building dates from the early eighteenth century, though parts go back to the seventeenth century. It replaces an even older tavern which stood on this site for many centuries.

Downstairs in the comfortable bar you'll find pictures of Old Birstall, but the real surprise is upstairs, now a restaurant. Here there are the fittings of an old courtroom, with magistrates box and a dock for prisoners' dock where local people were tried for minor offences.

Joseph Priestley

Birstall's main claim to fame is as the birthplace in 1733, at nearby Fieldhead, of Joseph Priestley, who discovered oxygen. It's worth taking a few minutes to walk into nearby Birstall marketplace to see the statue to Priestley.

The route from the Black Bull returns along Kirkgate to the church and takes a path on the left, through the second entrance to the extension to the graveyard opposite the church. This path goes through and below the main cemetery area, before turning left towards the newer part of the graveyard where it bears right into Church Woods, descending into a shallow, wooded ravine over a stile and footbridge. This path, almost certainly an ancient parishioners' way, is not shown on the Ordnance Map but is a popular permissive route in constant use. Keep ahead for about 50 metres to where the path forks. Take the path on the right which dips across the beck to stepping stones and up the bank to a stile in the fence. Cross the field to a broad gap in the hedge ahead, then turn left in the next field, rejoining the right of way from the Bradford Road.

This goes up a long field, the line of path marked by the remains of narrow stile posts, then alongside a fence before bearing right to join a short length of enclosed track. The path then swings to the right behind houses to reach a track which bears left around and in front of a bungalow onto the main A638 road at Gomersal.

Red House

Turn left for about 150 metres past a shop, houses and a chapel before crossing to Red House Museum, clearly signed, on the right. This handsome house, in its walled garden, was first built in the 1660s, unusually for its period, in brick, hence the name Red House. It was improved in the 18th century and became the home of the Taylor family, Spen Valley clothiers. In the 1830s Anne Taylor, school friend of Charlotte Brontë, lived there. Both Red House and Oakwell Hall, and members of the Taylor family in different personae, feature in "Shirley" – Charlotte's fascinating novel of the Spen Valley Luddites.

To emphasise the literary links, the house has been restored and recreated internally as it might well have appeared in 1832 when Charlotte was a frequent visitor to the Taylors. Period and reproduction furnishings, and lifelike models of Anne and her parents at work give an uncanny sense of time and place. Like Oakwell Hall, Red House is open daily.

Turn return to Oakwell. Go back up the main road to the point where the path from Birstall Church emerges by the bungalow, but this time fork left in front of the bungalow along a narrow enclosed path by a farm. It then runs along the edge of a field.

Keep directly ahead to the main road where a few metres to the left from where you emerge you'll see the entrance to the car park and bus stops, on the left to Bradford, across the road to Dewsbury.

17. LUDDENDEN DEAN

A walk with magnificent Pennine views to visit a secret valley and a Jacobean pub well known to Branwell Brontë.

Pub: The Lord Nelson, Luddenden. Webster's Green Label Bitter. Open: Monday to Saturday 1130 – 2300; Sunday 1200 – 1500 and 1900 – 2230. Food 1200 – 1400.

Start: Mytholmroyd

Distance: 7 miles (11 km)

Map: Ordnance Survey Outdoor Leisure Sheet 21 South Pennines. Landranger: Sheet 104

Public Transport: Frequent Metro Train service Caldervale Line (Manchester Victoria – Rochdale- Halifax-Bradford-Leeds; BR Table 40) to Mytholmrod, Sundays included.

By Car: Park in Mytholmroyd village – choice of well signed, free car parks.

Mytholmroyd lies on the junction of Calderdale and the tributary valley Cragg Vale, a busy, industrial settlement not without charm. Its greatest claim to fame is as the birthplace of poet laureate Ted Hughes, much of whose verse has been inspired by the Calderdale landscape.

The curious three-decker railway station is now sadly at the prey of mindless vandals. Walk in the Cragg Valley direction to the new Catholic church and the Good Shepherd on the left, at the rear of whose car park a track goes parallel to the railway alongside a factory. Follow this, soon passing scattered woodland and rising towards new houses. The public path continues alongside a wooden fence below the new garden rockeries before joining a broader track coming from the school. This is the drive to a largely rebuilt farmhouse, its garden and patio having been built over the public path. So keep straight ahead where behind the garden shed to the right beyond the house, where you'll find

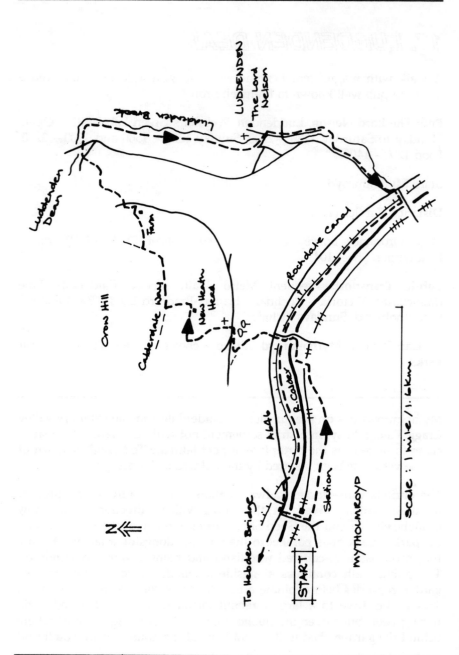

a small metal pedestrian gate. This leads to an attractive green path shelving along the hillside, and then gently downhill towards the railway line which is crossed at a metal bridge.

Follow the path past an old Baptist Chapel to the cross roads at Bierley where you turn left to cross a fine old bridge over the River Calder, then the canal bridge to the main road at Brearley (toilets here).

Packhorse Way

Cross and take the narrow track directly opposite Brearley Lane Top. Where the track forks take the narrow, enclosed track to the left which climbs steadily past the side of a wood. This old packhorse way is cobbled in places and has a causeway. You soon enjoy fine views along the valley. Ignore a gap stile into the wood on the right, but about 100 metres above the wood, before a bungalow ahead, stone steps in the hillside leads to a steep path along the wallside, then the edge of the wood above, to a wooden stile, almost a scramble at the top. Turn right here. To avoid this steep scramble, you can continue along the track to where it meets the lane by a farm and turn right in the lane uphill to the stile and bench; longer and with road walking, but less steep.

Continue past the junction with the road from Henden Bridge, and take the first narrow lane on the left which leads up past Midgeley's massive Methodist Chapel. The lane forks at a farm. Take the left fork onto a track around and outside the farm, climbing up to and through a gate to another junction of tracks. Turn right here, through another gate, now following a track running through gates above and behind the farm and towards New Heath Head, a palatial farm conversion overlooking the valley.

Just opposite its tennis courts, fork left into a broad green track keeping to the left of shallow ponds and springs. Climb up to the moor edge where, in the top right hand corner of the enclosure, a rickety wooden gate leads onto the moor.

The path, right, follows the wall along the moor edge. This is part of the Calderdale Way and you enjoy a quite superb panorama of Pennine moors: Stoodley Pike and its great memorial tower away to the west; Holme Moss television tower away to the south in the distance; and the deep and narrow Calder Valley serpenting its way between the vast, curving hills.

Crow Hill

Follow the path to a heather enclosure at the moorend where you bear left with the wire fence, magnificent views down into Luddenden valley below, a tall mill chimney into the foreground. The hill behind you is Crow Hill, described in a famous Ted Hughes poem.

Follow the path as it curves northwards, but take the next enclosed track on the right downhill through a gate and past a newly converted farmhouse to the lane. Turn left here along the lane, but where the lane bears left fork sharp right, signed as a bridleway, down another narrow, enclosed track between high stone walls. Ignore another track bearing off right to reach a terrace of cottages above a cobbled court. Proceed to the end of this where you'll see a narrow path sloping downhill enclosed between walls. This path can be a little overgrown in later summer and might have to be negotiated with care. It twists to the left down to Luddenden Dean, a superb, almost hidden, wooded valley.

Where the path emerges, cross almost opposite to a stile marked by a wooden sign to Goit Side, down steps and alongside a wall emerging on the lane opposite Booth Methodist Chapel. Cross and down the steps directly ahead, passing the graveyard down to Goit Side, a long row of Victorian terraces. Turn right here and go along the track in the bottom of the valley. At Booth, a collection of cottages, keep to the left of a narrow cottage on the main cobbled track. Ignore the next junction left and keep to the track along the valley bottom which curves gently past mill houses and shady gardens to yet another row of cottages. Straight ahead again here past another junction left, the lane now narrowing to a footpath which follows the side of the stream, Luddenden Beck.

Luddenden

You reach the entrance to Luddenden churchyard. Go through the gateway left, still alongside the stream on a richly evocative path by the Victorian stone footbridge to the graveyard and past the church itself into the centre of Luddenden.

Just to the right is The Lord Nelson Inn, with its proud datestone 1634. However, it was known as The White Swan prior to the Battle of Trafalgar in 1805. The pub was reputedly haunted, but its ghost was duly exorcised. There's a tombstone built in a chimney where a local Squire supposedly hanged himself. There are also stories of secret passages. It was here that Branwell Brontë drank with his cronies when he worked as ticket clerk on the new Leeds-Manchester Railway at the long vanished station at Luddenden Foot. Apart from some new paint and a new sign, Branwell would still recognise this seventeenth century pub with its dark, quite genuine oak beams and very Pennine atmosphere. This is very much a pub for the local community rather than a tourist destination. There is a small enclosed beer garden.

Turn right outside the pub door, passing the church, going right again into High Street past the Post Office and Working Men's Club to a second road junction. Directly ahead is a curious half-stone half-brick electricity substation just to the right and beyond which you'll see a narrow enclosed path between the hillside and a recently demolished mill. Take this as it follows the valley down, again going into an attractive area of oakwoods before you bear right at a fork to the little humpback bridge on the right over Luddenden Beck leading up steps between houses to the main road.

Turn left here, and follow the road for about 600 metres down to its junction with the main A646 Calder Valley road where immediately to the left Thwaite's fans will find the Weavers' Arms with excellent Thwaite's Bitter on offer.

Otherwise cross at the pedestrian crossing to turn right into Station Road, the name recalling Branwell's long lost station, turning left immediately over the canal bridge onto the towpath of the Rochdale Canal. Just over a mile and a half of brisk walking (allow half an hour) and pleasant canal scenery, even a couple of locks, will bring you into Mytholmroyd on the main road. Straight ahead (cross to the broader pavement) to the cross roads and car parks. Turn left along the Cragg Vale road back to the station.

18. ROBINWOOD

An upper Calderdale walk which offers some striking scenery and a chance to sample locally brewed ale.

Pub: The Staff of Life, Lydgate, Todmorden. Robinwood Best Bitter, XB, Old Fart, Timothy Taylor Best and Landlord. Open: Mondays to Saturdays 1200 – 1500 and 1900 – 2300 hours. Sundays 1200 – 1500 hours and 1900 – 2230 hours.

Start: Todmorden Railway Station

Distance: 5 miles (8 km)

Map: Ordnance Survey Outdoor Leisure Sheet 21 South Pennines; Landranger Sheet 103

Public Transport: Hourly Metro Train service Calderdale Line (Leeds-Halifax-Rochdale-Manchester Victoria BR Table 40) to Todmorden. Yorkshire Rider buses from Halifax, Rochdale, Burnley.

By Car: Park in Todmorden – car park at station.

Todmorden stands at the cross roads of Lancashire and Yorkshire. The boundary between the Red and White Rose Counties once lay along the beck which runs underneath the Town Hall, leaving the sculptor on the frieze above its neo-classical colonnade to include woolsacks on the eastern side, cotton bales on the west.

Todmorden

It's a town of immense character. Its streets, often torturously narrow and steep, climb and twist steep hillsides that surround the town, terraces at often steep angles or in rows like dominos. The dark, often sombre gritstone of the moors reflected in the mills, chapels, streets of the town itself and its outlying communities. Yet the moortops, vast and empty except for a few old farms, seem to occupy a different world, the haunt of curlew and lapwing.

From Todmorden Station entrance, turn left down the station drive and left again under the railway arch. Almost immediately out of the tunnel, look for steep steps on the right past that climb the hillside the gable end of houses, Ridge Steps. Go up these to Well Lane, turning right but where Well Lane slopes away downhill to the right, take the path by the metal fence and below a grassy slope straight ahead.

This leads into beautiful oak and beech woods, above Centre Vale Park. Follow this track as it contours the hillside with fine views, finally dipping slightly to join a lane.

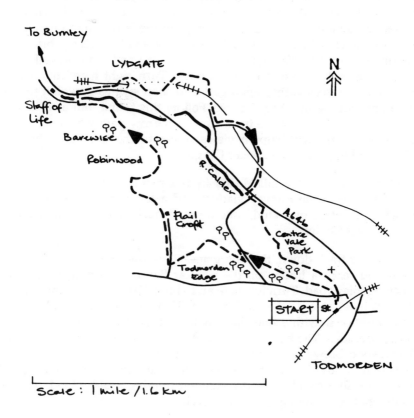

Calderdale Way

Turn left here, walking uphill for about 80 metres to where a narrow path, signed the Calderdale Way, climbs sharp right steeply uphill through the woods, up a series of steps. Take your time until the path finally levels out contouring the hillside, again with fine views back across Todmorden, before turning sharp left through a stile, alongside a fieldwall to a second stile and into an enclosed lane. Follow this up to its junction with a farm track at Todmorden Edge.

Turn right here, along a straight track by the farm which now descends gently towards a renovated Jacobean farmhouse, Flail Croft. As you approach the farm, look for a narrow grassy path on your left which follows the wallside along a grassy bank above the track. This soon swings away left to a stile by a gate beyond the farm. Go through here to join the track which swings left around a shallow gorge, bridging a streamlet, and, enclosed between a ruined wall and the fieldwall, rise to a junction with a second enclosed track. Turn right here, into a green way which descends through a gate and soon swings downhill through a natural cutting in a broad curve. Follow this round, but as it hairpins back to the right, leave the track along a narrow path which cuts across the slope, again with superb views across to the trees of Robinwood ahead, and beyond into Cliviger Gorge.

Look for a stile in the hillside ahead at a point on the opposite side of the valley from the railway viaduct and a large stone mill. This leads down stone steps of a kind, onto a broad track along a shelf above the infant River Calder.

Follow this track down, through gates, along the river side. Keep ahead until you reach a bridge on the right at Barewise leading to the main A646 Burnley road. Turn left here and about 150 metres up the road, on the left hand side, is the Staff of Life. This end of terrace pub is small and traditional with stone flag floors and paraphernalia dating from earlier decades. The bar is a delight for there are beers from the nearby Robinwood brewery and often a guest beer. Having been in the Good Beer Guide now it attracts visitors from afar but this is a locals' pub. There is also a small seafood restaurant offering healthy food, with the well-kept beers waiting for your arrival.

The Staff of Life

From the Staff of Life return along the main road for about 400 metres to the centre of Lydgate. You might, if looking for interesting Calderdale pubs, consider searching out the delightful Poultry Dealers Arms, at the far end of the village beyond the Robinwood brewery where there is a good pint of Boddington's and a very friendly Todmorden welcome.

Otherwise, turn left under the viaduct up Jump's Road, a lane which curves sharply to the right back underneath the railway viaduct in a spectacular fashion climbing to the village school. At the fork just past the school, take the higher track to the left. At the next junction by a curious, single storey building take the left fork which leads to a lovely path which contours around the hillside through woodland over the railway tunnel to emerge in a stony track.

Centre Vale Park

Turn right here back under the railway yet again, but at the housing estate take a narrow, unsurfáced track which climbs steeply uphill to join a road. Turn right past houses, looking for steps past bungalows, on the right which join a road leading back under the railway and alongside a large, red brick mill. Follow this road back to the main A646 turning left and crossing to enter Centre Vale Park. Turn left and following park paths make your way to the far right exit in the direction of town. There are toilets here and once under the railway arch you return to the station entrance at Todmorden.

19. CLIVIGER

A walk through one of the largest parishes in the country between Holme Chapel, and Hurstwood. There are several patches of rough ground and one or two climbs but this is a most satisfying walk.

Pub: The Queen Hotel, Cliviger (the village is known as Holme Chapel but some refer to it as Cliviger which also happens to be the name of the parish). Monday to Saturday 1100 – 1500 except Wednesday. Evenings 1900 – 2300. Sundays 1200 – 1500 and 1900 – 2230.

Distance: 8 miles (13 km)

Maps: Pathfinder Sheets 690 Rawtenstall and Hebden Bridge, 681 Burnley. Landranger 103 Blackburn.

Public Transport: There is a regular weekday bus service from Burnley, Todmorden and Rochdale using buses 589 or 592. Hourly on Sundays. Telephone (Burnley) 831263 for details.

By Car: Cliviger is on the A646 between Burnley and Todmorden. There is limited on street parking in the village, which is also known as Holme.

The Queen Hotel, dating from 1863 according to the date stone on the end gable of the building, is one of two public houses remaining in the village, the other being The Ram. The Queen looks after ramblers seriously for outside the door is a shoe and boot cleaner. Inside is a warm welcome in this traditional Lancashire public house. In the hall is an early model of a Singer sewing machine and a basket of wood for the fire. The first door on the left leads into one of the two lounge rooms situated either side of a central bar.

The publicans and some of the locals go walking themselves, so appreciate the need that walkers have for refreshment. Currently on offer is Websters bitter and Ruddles County on handpull and for those seeking food, sandwiches are available on request. As with most pubs mentioned in this book, well-behaved children are welcome. The old pictures on the wall reflect aspects of life in the last century and in the

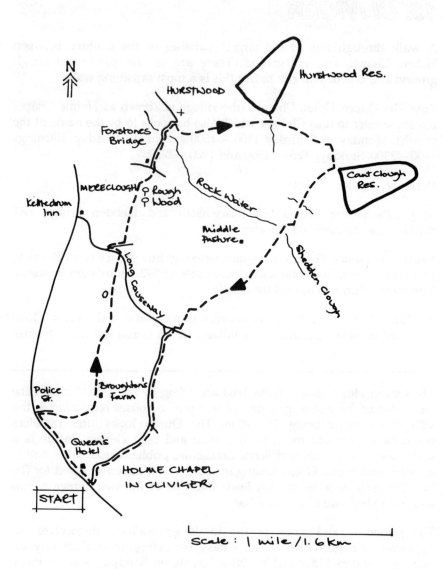

Scale : 1 mile / 1.6 km

earlier decades of this one. They feature textile production, weaving and also the village social outing. There is even a picture of a steam-hauled train stopping at Holme station earlier in the century. Regrettably, there is no station now for the sprinters to stop at while journeying across the Pennines.

Wool

Villagers used to be partly employed in wool production at local farmsteads about, then turned to spinning cotton yarns and cloths in these moorland edge communities. The transportation of such goods was also an important activity but the gorge of Cliviger had something of a bad reputation with early travellers as there were so many witches and robbers on the roads. Many a tale was told in local hostelries.

One local family, the Whitakers, who became prominent in Lancashire, took a real interest in the environment for one of the Whitakers living in the eighteenth century planted an estimated 422000 young trees hereabouts. The parish was a far busier place one hundred years ago than today for there was a corn mill, fulling mill and small scale mining. Agriculture, nevertheless, still retained its importance and each year the Ram Fair and other local sheep sales drew the farming community for miles around.

Start the ramble from the Queen Hotel. Turn right and walk along the main road to pass a row of houses. Before the police station, turn right up Grange road as signposted towards an old farm. Before the gates, bear slightly right through a gateway and ahead to a wicket gate just beyond the garden. Go through it and head up the hillside, to the left of the old building, and through wet ground. As you climb further up the bank look for a gateway on the brow of the hill. Once through, keep ahead virtually parallel to the fence on the right as it leads up to Broughton's farm.

Before the farm, keep slightly left heading through a gap in the broken wall to the wood's edge and then the path dips down to a stream and winds up to a stile set in a gateway. Keep ahead through a narrow field to a gap stile by another gate and then turn right to go directly ahead, ie not on the track coming in from the left or right. The path leads across the field through broken walls guarding an old track and to a gap stile in the next intact drystone wall.

About half a mile from here is The Kettledrum Inn at Mereclough, featured in The Good Beer Guide for years. It is a possible stop for those who happen to be thirsty already. For those who are going to seek it out, turn left along the track and follow it to the main road at Mereclough and turn right. The Kettledrum, named after a Derby winner in the last century, is well known for its food and has a range of guest beers. The ramble can be regained by walking up the Long Causeway, the road which climbs into the hills from the pub. Alternatively, a bus can be caught back to Cliviger; it passes the pub.

Long Causeway

For those soldiering on, keep ahead, passing a pool on the left, to another stile and straight on again to cross the next wall by way of a step stile. Now, head for a point between the gateway and house ahead, for the step stile in the wall is not discernible at first. This exits onto the Long Causeway, a busy road, so please take care. Cross it and turn left for the short distance to the corner. The Long Causeway is said by some to be a highway dating from Bronze Age times, ie well over 3000 years ago. Others are more inclined to suggest that it was mediaeval.

Rock Water

This is the corner where Kettledrum diversionists rejoin the route. Turn right up the track and once past the entrance to a house on the left look for a step stile on the left and cross it. Walk along the short walled path to cross another stile at the rear of a garage. In the field, head directly ahead rather than left or right and you eventually see a gate leading to a track which winds down a little valley. Very shortly, it curves right then slightly left. Leave the track to go over a stile by another gate here, leading into a pasture. Walk down the field keeping close to the wall on the left and go through a gate onto a track. To the right is the Rock Water Bird Conservation Centre, a sanctuary for both endangered and common species of birds including pheasants, poultry, pigeons and foreign varieties. It is open all year from 1000 am until dusk all year (except December and January).

Hurstwood

Turn left and then almost immediately right to pass by a farmhouse and farm buildings. The track peters into a lovely green lane and down to Foxstones bridge over a brook known as Rock Water and up to the hamlet of Hurstwood, described as 'More of a farmyard than a village street'. This is a piece of Tudor England with Tattersall's house, Hurstwood hall and Spenser's cottage, associated with the poet Edmund Spenser, who visited his uncle here on many occasions. Richard Tattersall also hailed from these parts, the person responsible for introducing the "Tattersall's of Knightsbridge" and Newmarket, world known stables and horse dealers.

Spenser's cottage

Fairies

Peaceful though the area seems now nearby is the site of the Battle of Brunanburgh (Althelstan leading Wessex and Mercian warriors against the rest in the Dark Ages). The bloody battle was fought on the banks of the Brun drawing its waters from surrounding moors. Strangely enough, the area known is also renowned for its legends such as fairies milking cows, and tiny pats of butter at nearby wells.

At the road go right and at the junction right again and right over the bridge and towards the car park. However, turn left beforehand to pass through a green gate and by a house. The lane rises gently between trees towards Hurstwood reservoir, built in 1925 to serve the needs of the East Lancashire population. Before reaching it, your path is signposted to the right, through the woodland, over a water feeder channel and through a kissing gate.

Walk out onto moorland, through old earthworks. Re-join the track ahead as it climbs more steeply. Towards the summit, ignore the lesser track ahead but curve right and descend to a stile and gate by Cant Clough reservoir built in the 1870s. The view across the reservoir to Worsthorne moor is dramatic, especially when the wind cuts up the water on a bright Spring day.

Once over the stile, follow the road ahead, rather than along the embankment wall. After the first wall boundary cut off left and head slightly left down the steep bank towards the brook, looking for a large boulder near the banks which acts as a marker. Pass this and then ford the stream where the boundary walls meet the stream.

Limestone Hushings

On the other side, follow the wall, which should be on your right, out of the clough and onto moorland. There are very few landmarks to follow in this isolated stretch of path which is ill defined. Pass an old stone gateway at first, then descend gently towards a stream across very wet ground keeping as near as possible to the broken wall. This curves around to a wire fence where you will see a stile on the left. Do not cross this but instead walk down to the stream in Shedden clough. This area used to be quarried for limestone and the remains of these small workings, known as limestone hushings, can be seen around you.

Once across, keep ahead through scrub and rock and follow another drystone wall out of the clough. Just as you begin to feel lost a stile appears in the top left corner. Cross this and then keep ahead to meet a track, turn right and then left over a stile. Go slightly left to pass near the ruins of old farm buildings and cross another stile. In the next field, cross the wet ground heading slightly right and then the path curves right as waymarked.

Green Lane

In the next very large field, follow the field wall on your right at first but then begin to walk slightly left over rough ground beyond the electricity pylon towards a tall ladder stile which soon comes into view. Cross this and keep ahead for a short distance before going left and through a gateway towards a farm. Cross a stile by a gate and as you approach the farm take the right fork to join the road. Turn right and walk for a very short distance before crossing the road and walking down a lane by Pottery farm and by another set of buildings before the road gives out onto a wide green lane. Follow this down the hillside until it reaches a junction where you'll find a fine seat to rest awhile. Go left here into Holme Chapel to exit on the main road near The Ram pub.

This green lane does have parallel paths for part of its length as evidenced by stiles from time to time. Once back in Holme, turn right for The Queen.

20. HEPTONSTALL AND HARDCASTLE CRAGS

A walk to be enjoyed at any time of the year, but never finer than in late autumn when the colours of the Hardcastle Crag woodlands are a theatrical blaze of colour.

Pub: The Cross, Heptonstall. Timothy Taylor's Landlord, Bitter and Golden Best. Open Monday to Saturday 1130 – 1600 and 1900 – 2300. Sunday 1200 – 1500 and 1900 – 2230. Bar snacks available.

Start: Hebden Bridge Station

Distance: 8 miles (13k)

Maps: Ordnance Survey Outdoor Leisure Sheet 21 South Pennines; Landranger sheet 103 Blackburn.

Public transport: Metro Train Hebden Bridge (Calderdale or Roses Link); frequent buses (590, 591) from Halifax and Rochdale. Metro Day Rover valid.

By Car: Choice of car parks in Hebden Bridge. Join the route from the Information Centre in the town centre.

Hebden Bridge has taken upon itself the role of unofficial "capital" of the South Pennines, thanks to its position in mid Calderdale, with cottages crowing along the valley sides like some kind of inland Pennine version of a Cornish or East Coast fishing village. Note, on this walk, the curious "double deck" terraces built on the hillside to save space. This former textile town, home (in Nutclough Mill) of the world's first producer co-operative, now enjoys a reputation as a tourist centre. There are horse-drawn trips from the marina on the newly restored Rochdale Canal, and an excellent choice of shops, pubs and restaurants in the revitalised town centre.

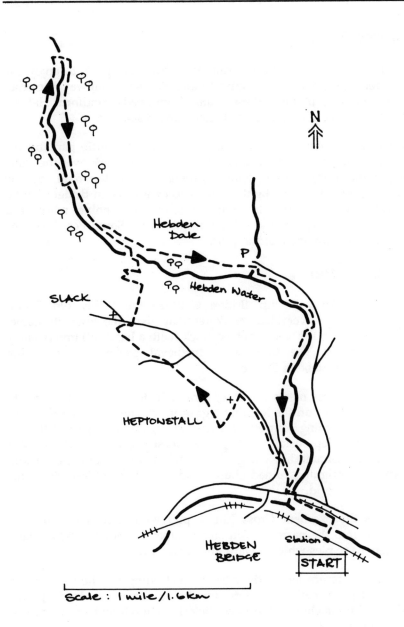

N

Hebden Dale

P

Hebden Water

SLACK

HEPTONSTALL

HEBDEN BRIDGE

Station

START

Scale : 1 mile/1.6km

Restored Station

Another reason for arriving by train at Hebden Bridge is to enjoy the town's perfectly preserved Lancashire and Yorkshire Railway Victorian Station, served by frequent diesel trains from Leeds, Bradford, Halifax, Rochdale, Manchester, Blackburn, Preston and Blackpool.

Turn left at the bottom of the station drive into the little park by the canal, going across the concrete bridge at the end of park over the canal leading into pleasant town centre gardens. Across the road, by the Yorkshire Bank and traffic lights, is the excellent Hebden Bridge Tourist Information Centre with its excellent stock of Pennine maps and guidebooks, and displays and exhibitions about the South Pennines. The Centre is open daily most of the year.

Hebden Water

From the Centre walk up Bridge Gate to the lovely old Tudor hump-back bridge over Hebden Water that gives the town its name. Cross, climbing up the steep cobbled track (with a handrail) immediately opposite. This is The Buttress, a medieval packhorseway linking Heptonstall with Hebden Bridge.

Where The Buttress meets the lane, turn right for about 100 metres to locate narrow steps on the left that zigzag up the hillside, superb views of the town rewarding your effort. Turn right again at the lane at the top and walk into Heptonstall, perhaps the finest surviving example of a pre-industrial Pennine hill village. There are weavers' cottages, a Cloth Hall and an intriguing ruined church and one of the oldest Methodist Chapels in the world.

It also has the excellent Cross Inn, a pub with stone bay windows looking out into the narrow main street, superb .Timothy Taylor's beer and home made pies which reward any weary walker.

From the pub, return left to the cross roads leading to a housing estate. Take the flagged path and steps on the corner which leads to the abandoned Tudor church, the later Victorian church and the Grammar School (now a small museum).

Hot Coals

The churchyard of the older church is full of atmosphere, the roofless ruins like some strange monument to long forgotten communities of hillfarmers and weavers who struggled for an existence in a hostile Pennine environment. Many gravestones only bear initials as families were too poor to have full names and dates inscribed. David Hartley one of the notorious Cragg Vale coiners, is buried here. Hartley was hanged at York for "clipping" gold coins of the realm to steal the metal. It is said that the Cross Inn at Heptonstall was frequented by these same coiners who reputedly murdered an informer by pouring hot coals down his trousers!

Leave by the gate at the top left hand corner of the churchyard by the Victorian church. Continue on the dirt track ahead past houses, and bear right at a fork by garages to follow the Calderdale Way signs along a narrow enclosed track. You emerge at a magnificent viewpoint across the wooded Colden valley below, the tower of Stoodley Pike prominent across the main Calder Valley on the horizon canal, turnpike road and railway intertwining through the valley floor, mill chimneys in the foreground. There is no better view to evoke the Pennines heritage.

Your way is sharp right, a narrow, rocky path through heather and eventually scattered woodland, along the top of the ravine close to the wall. Keep in the same direction until the path joins a narrow lane. Descend left for about 100 metres before bearing off right along another enclosed path which now climbs uphill, eventually emerging behind the hamlet of Slack. Turn right between houses to emerge near the cross roads to Burnley and an imposing Ebenezer Chapel.

Walk for a short distance back towards Heptonstall, but look for a footpath on the left by the side of a cottage known as Waterloo. This leads to a narrow path which zigzags, thrillingly, into Hebden Dale in the centre of the magnificent 400 acre National Trust woodlands of Hardcastle Crags.

Gibson Mill

Follow the path down past the Scout Adventure Centre to where stepping stones cross the stream, Hebden Water. Cross and turn left along the riverside path which eventually emerges at Gibson Mill, a late eighteenth century former cotton spinning mill named after its founder Abraham Gibson. Turn left at the mill, over the bridge, and take the path immediately on the right which leads between and round the old mill ponds, eventually going along the riverside before joining a forest track climbing away from the valley floor. At a fork of tracks follow the track right green waymarked posts along the path that hairpins down to the river and a footbridge. Cross to join a broad track. Turn right here, soon passing gritstone outcrops deep in the oakwoods which are the actual "Crags" that give the area its name.

Follow the main track back past Gibson Mill continuing in the same direction to the Lodge and car park at the estate entrance. Immediately beyond here, turn right over the bridge, following the wooden signs and yellow waymarks back to Hebden Bridge. The route turns left past Midgehole Working Men's Club and along the riverside, crosses a bridge to a gate, going left to the lane. Turn right in the lane, but go up steps into a wood parallel to a lane.

Rejoin the lane down the path which leads parallel to the lane before turning right back to the riverside past a bungalow. Go over another footbridge by the bowling green, along the riverbank by a cricket ground, to a stile and yet another bridge. Walk straight ahead here before swinging right to a final bridge, bearing right before almost immediately turning sharp left into Hangingstone Lane which leads to Hebden Bridge town centre.

21. STANBURY

A short walk in Brontë country, easily fitted into an afternoon, and using some intriguing paths and packhorseways well away from the usual over-frequented tourist trails.

Pubs: The Friendly, Stanbury. Bass, Stone's Bitter. Open Monday to Friday 1100 – 2300; 1100 – 1600 and 1900-2300 in Winter. Sunday 1200 – 1500 and 1900 – 2230. Food 1200 – 2000 in summer; 1200 – 1430 in winter.

The Fleece, Main Street, Haworth. Clark's Landlord, Bitter, Golden Best. Open 1130 – 2300 in summer; 1130 – 1500 and 1900 – 2300 in Winter on Monday to Saturday. Sundays 1200 – 1500 hours and 1900 – 2230 hours. Food available.

Start: Haworth Station (Keighley and Worth Valley Railway)

Distance: 4 miles (7 km)

Maps: OS Outdoor Leisure Sheet 21 The South Pennines; Landranger Sheet 103 Blackburn.

Public Transport: Metro Train on the Airedale line to Keighley (BR Table 36) then Keighley Worth Valley Railway (Timetable Tel 0535 45214) or Bus 665 to Haworth. Metro Day Rover tickets not valid on KWVR but discount for Day Rover ticket holders.

By Car: Haworth is often congested at weekends and holiday times, at such times it is recommended to use the park and ride from Ingrow (see below). Otherwise use one of several car parks in the village and join the route at Haworth church.

There's more to Haworth than the Brontës. If you want to really get the feel of the place, go out of season to get something of that early industrial revolution atmosphere which survives under the tinsel trappings of tourism, cobbled streets, stone courtyards and cottages in a magnificent moorland setting.

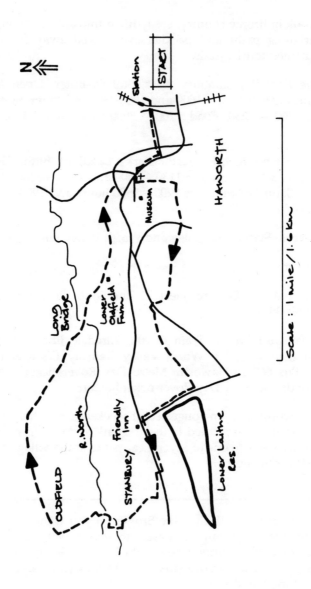

N

Station

START

HAWORTH

Museum

Long Bridge

Lower Oldfield Farm

R. North

Friendly Inn

OLDFIELD

STANBURY

Lower Laithe Res.

Scale : 1 mile / 1.6 Km

Travel there by train, if you can, from Keighley on the spectacular little Worth Valley Steam Railway. Motorists can leave their cars at the award-winning park-and-ride station at Ingrow on the Halifax road out of Keighley, with time to visit the excellent new Carriage Museum. If the train isn't running, there are frequent buses to Haworth from Keighley Bus station.

The walk starts from Haworth Station. Cross the footbridge to the village side of the tracks, and walk up Butt Lane directly ahead, climbing its stone setts between the Park and the School.

At the main road cross directly ahead to continue along Butt Lane which bears right to climb into West Street, Haworth's famous cobbled main street, lined with tea, souvenir and antique shops. Turn left near the summit, immediately beyond the church and go along the cobbled alleyway towards the Parsonage, but just past the church go left again along the narrow, flagged and enclosed path below the graveyard signed Haworth Moor. Keep ahead through the kissing-gate and past the top car park to a junction of paths. Now turn right on a broader, enclosed and stony track which climbs past a couple of gentrified farm houses to join the road past Penistone Hill Country Park.

Cross, but do not take the waymarked path towards Withins and the Brontë Falls ahead. Your path is slightly right over a patch of tarmac along an unwaymarked, broad green track through the heather. Follow it over the moor crest, with fine views across Lower Laithe Reservoir and the Upper Worth Valley ahead until the stone cemetery wall with its enclosed trees comes into view on the right. At a crossways past the far corner of the wall, take the track right down to the lane where it emerges opposite a parking place. Cross the rough grass to pick up a green track slanting down the slope ahead. Follow it left, past the reservoir water treatment works to emerge on the Stanbury road at the dam.

Stanbury

Turn right, cross the dam and walk uphill to the road junction and left for quarter of a mile into Stanbury with its variety of remarkable 18th houses and weavers' cottages. It was in this village that Timothy Feather, the last of the old Pennine handloom weavers who carried on his craft from an old loom in his cottage almost to his death in the early years of this century. For those who are interested, you can see old Timmy's loom in Cliffe Castle Museum, Keighley.

The second of the two pubs receives our special recommendation, the well named Friendly Inn, a cosy, traditional Pennine village hostelry, with an old fashioned central bar serving both lounge and tap room, a well kept pint of Stone's and good home cooked food.

Griffe Mill

From the Friendly, continue in the same direction but turn right past the white cottage about 20 metres beyond the pub, into an unsurfaced track which runs behind the village. Turn left to where the track swings into a farmyard. Your way is now sharply to the right, past farm outbuildings and down the hillside pasture. Look for a line of broken wall below. Walk to its left as it becomes a sunken green lane, rather muddy but enclosed, (the remains of the wall provides dry footing). It curves round the high wall surrounding the melancholy ruins of Griffe Mill, a long vanished water-powered worsted mill.

The path goes around the mill to a stile on the left leading to the bridge across the River Worth and past the remains of the old mill pond. Follow a faint green track uphill by the wallside to Oldfield House Farm. Don't take the track right here, but go right through a crude wooden kissing gate stile in the wall corner above the junction, and follow a path along the bottom of a field to another stile.

The path enters a farmyard bearing slightly right along a track to another stile left, this time past a garden. Keep in the same direction over stiles, with the wall to your right, across a field to locate a wooden stile below the farm directly ahead. The way is very slightly to the left, still marked by stiles, to a junction with another crossing track. Ignore this, but keep ahead to a green way which slopes right down pass another farmhouse and a ladder stile. Follow this green way, Street Lane, down to a beautiful little wooded gill and waterfall. Go over more stiles, but where the way opens out into a broad field, your path is to the right, through a field gate back across the stream before following the streamside down to the River Worth to cross at a beautiful single arch packhorse bridge, Long Bridge.

Lower Oldfield Farm

Take the enclosed track uphill which leads to Lower Oldfield Farm at a ladder stile. Turn left along the track outside the farm which ends at a stile into a narrow enclosed way. Keep ahead, over more stiles to the top of a long field where a stile on the left indicates the continuation of the path. Follow it between the walls of a Chapel cemetery to emerge at North Street in Haworth village. Cross and take the first turn right along the cobbled street to rejoin West Street by the Tourist Information Centre.

About half way down on the left hand side you'll find the Fleece, a tall early 19th century building whose Timmy Taylor's Golden Best is memorable, not to mention the Bitter and the Landlord. Enjoy the spoof Brontë exhibition in the Lounge.

22. GOOSEYE

Secret valleys and high pastures in central Airedale.

Pubs: The Turkey Inn, Gooseye. Tetley's Bitter, Burton Bitter, Turkey Bitter. Open Monday to Friday 1200 – 1500 (except Mondays) and 1730 – 2300; Saturday 1200 – 1700 and 1900 – 2300; Sunday 1200 – 1500 and 1900-2230. Food daily 1200 – 1430 and 1830-2100.

The Grinning Rat, Church Street, Keighley. Old Mill Bitter, Taylor's Landlord, Moorhouses Pendle Witches Brew, Mitchell's Bitter and ESB, plus nine constantly changing guest beers including a dark mild and stout or porter. Open Monday to Saturday 1100 – 2300, Sunday 1200 – 1500 and 1900 – 2300. Food 1200 – 1500.

Start: Steeton Top cross roads.

Distance: 5 miles (8 km)

Maps: Pathfinder sheet 671; Landranger sheet 104 Leeds.

Public Transport: Keighley & District 666, 668, 712, 762, 765 from Keighley to Steeton Top. Metrotrain Airedale Line (BR Table 36) to Steeton and Silsden station (400 metres from Steeton cross roads). Return from Keighley.

By Car: Park at Keighley and travel to Steeton by train or bus as above.

Steeton is a deceptive village, with quiet and interesting corners away from the main road. The Old Star Inn by the traffic lights, has an excellent reputation for its well kept Courage Director's and hand-pulled John Smith's Magnet might attract certain ramblers at the start of this walk, though temptation enough lies in store.

If you arrive by train at Steeton Station, follow the old main road, now the station drive, to join the Keighley road up to the traffic lights at Steeton Top.

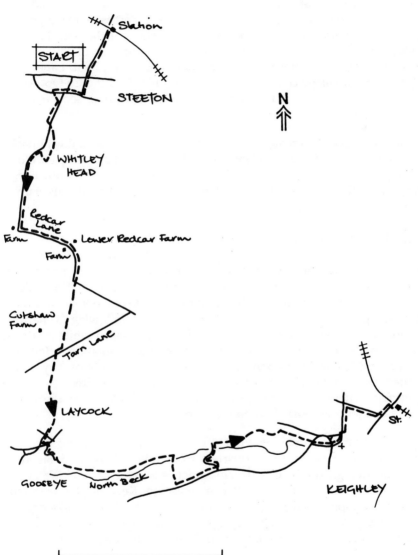

Scale: 1 mile / 1.6 km

From the traffic lights at Steeton Top make your way alongside the Goat's Head and up School Street which soon becomes an enclosed way past the primary school. Do not go up the steps at the end, but bear right, behind the school and into an attractive courtyard of cottages and a house with a 1710 datestone, continuing into Hollin Bank Lane. Turn right, into the village centre, past the lower Green and the Co-Op. As the road bends left, keep straight ahead along Chapel Road, soon reaching the high Green.

Turn left across this green, following the line if a hollow pathway past a bench that climbs to join the lane above, Dale View. Turn left past Worth Photograph Processors into Barrow Lane. Turn right and walk uphill, keeping to the right hand side to face oncoming traffic on this narrow lane.

Steeton Beck

About 150 metres above the large mill on the left, look for some steps marked with a footpath sign which lead to a public path. This follows the top of a mill dam and winds round the outside of a derelict millpond and along the millrace, passing stables before following a narrow, wooded valley where a stream, Steeton Beck, tumbles in white cataracts. You soon go underneath a road bridge; avoid the temptation to follow a path round to the bridge and road, but keep on the right of way which carries on as a faint path up the side of the stream almost to a top waterfall, where it hairpins round and curves back up to the hedge above and joins a house drive to the road.

Turn left past the hamlet of Whitley Head, a row of moorland cottages. You now have about three quarters of a mile of unavoidable road walking, though the lane is usually quiet, and ever finer views across Airedale are more than adequate compensation. Keep on the main lane Redcar Lane, past a cross roads, steadily climbing a low broad ridge. At White Field Farm it bears left, giving panoramic views across Airedale to Rombalds Moor with the mill town of Silsden in the foreground.

Continue past Middle and Lower Redcar Farms, bearing right with the lane for another 300 metres but at the next bend in he road there is a stile and waymarked path almost at the corner. Cross, and keep in the same direction to a gate in the field wall ahead, beyond which you will see a gap stile in the wall ahead. The path now bears diagonally right over to a stone step stile in the corner of the pasture. Keep in the same direction to a stile in the corner of the next field, and again to where the path, at a signpost, joins Tarn Lane by the entrance to Cutshaw Farm.

Turn right here for 40 metres to locate a gap stile on the left (not signed) where the path continues again to the right hand corner of the field. Keep in the same direction through a series of stiles between long narrow fields and, eventually, as the rooftops of Laycock village come into view, bear slightly left. The line of stiles eventually bearsg across to the bottom right hand corner of a large field close to the village, from where an enclosed fieldtrack through a gate leads into the centre of Laycock.

Laycock

Walk through the village with its fine seventeenth and eighteenth century cottages and farmhouses. At the Old Post House (former post office) with a letter box in the wall, bear left along what looks like a private cobbled drive in front of some impressive four storey weavers' cottages. This ist a narrow enclosed pedestrian way, with tall lamp standards, which emerges at a stile on the steep lane down to the curious hamlet of Gooseye.

Gooseye

This remarkable mill hamlet lies in a deep, almost hidden, fold of the hills formed by the North Beck. The Turkey Mill, a paper mill long since closed, has been converted to residential accommodation, but the village inn, The Turkey Inn, thrives. The pub was long famous for its Gooseye Bitter, which sadly is no longer brewed, though a successor, only available at the Turkey Inn, Turkey Bitter, is highly recommended. There is a good Pennine feel to the pub which serves a wide choice of food at lunchtimes and evenings, but save yourself a walk down the long hill if it is Monday lunchtime when it closes.

Leaving the Turkey Inn at Gooseye is always a struggle, especially when faced with the steep climb back to Laycock. Look out for the stile and ginnel which cuts off the corner back to the centre of Laycock village, where if the hill is too much for you there is a regular minibus service (weekdays) into Keighley. Otherwise, less than 100 metres on the right, is your track, well signposted for Holme House Wood and Fell Lane. In common with the rest of Bradford, it is marked in kilometres and not miles and it leads back down to the valley bottom. Note the interesting spring-fed horse trough on the trackside, a relic when this track served another mill. Where the track bends right, your way is over the stile, left and between wall and fence to join an attractive riverside path alongside the North beck, soon going through a wooded area. Take care over several small sikes feeding into the main stream. At a footbridge cross the stream and follow a faint flagged path by the remains of a hedge uphill to reach Fell Lane.

Fell Lane

Turn left in Fell Lane (again buses into Keighley), with cottages on the left and modern houses on the right, for some 500 metres past a modern pub. At Holme Mill Lane turn left past bungalows, following what becomes the drive to Holme Mill, now Stell's paper tube manufacturers. Turn right at the mill entrance down a footpath alongside the wire perimeter fence, across a footbridge over the stream and up steps. At a junction of tracks, turn right between ramshackle allotment buildings and smallholdings, with fascinating views of the river and fine mill scenery across the valley, including the massive rectangular bulk of the Pennine Weavers' mill.

The track eventually bears left past new housing up to the road. Go right for about 80 metres before turning down right again in front of Crimea Terrace. Bear left past 1960s flats, opposite a new school. Keep ahead to a junction of paths. Your route now dips to the right, along a tarmac path through woodland. Pass the GPO sorting office and another fine mill, complete with clock, at the far side of the river, and a curious riverside garden. Cross the main road directly ahead and walk down Damside to the Halifax road, emerging at the Jet Garage. Cross once again, now bearing slightly left into Church Street, at the end of which is the Grinning Rat, a real ale drinkers' paradise: a jolly, exuberant pub, with converted sewing machine tables, a choice of bars, oodles of atmosphere (Blues Nights Thursdays) and barrels of real ale.

Bus and rail stations are three and eight minutes' walk away respectively.

23. SUNNYDALE

From remarkable 18th century canal engineering to high moorland farms and seventeenth century weaving villages and early industrial settlements, all linked by footpaths rich in interest.

Pub: The Old Queen's Head, Main Street, Bingley. Webster's Yorkshire Bitter, Wilson's, Ruddles County and a variety of guest real ales. Open Monday, Tuesday, Wednesday and Thursday 1130 – 1500 and 1900 – 2300; Fridfay and Saturday 1100 – 2300; Sunday 1200 – 1500 and 1900 – 2230. Food daily 1200 – 1900.

Start: Bingley Station

Distance: 8 miles (13 km)

Maps: Pathfinder Sheets 671, 682; Landranger Sheet 104 Leeds.

Public Transport: Frequent rail services (Sundays included), Metro Train Airedale Line from Leeds and Bradford Forster Square to Skipton (BR Table 36). Yorkshire Rider Buses 760 from Leeds, 665, 666 from Bradford.

By Car: Park in Bingley – large pay car park immediately behind the station (start of walk).

If you arrive at Bingley's fine old Midland Railway Station from a train from Leeds or Bradford, cross by the vast steps and footbridge to the opposite platform and out into the car park behind the station from where steps by the Waterbus stop (an alternative way of getting to Bingley in the summer months) lead onto the canal towpath. Turn right under Park Road Bridge soon reaching Three Rise Locks and not far beyond, the famous Five Rise Locks.

Five Rise Locks

These twin "staircase" locks were built in 1774 by four local masons employed by the Leeds and Liverpool Canal Company under the supervision of Chief Engineer John Longbotham. The Five Rise Locks

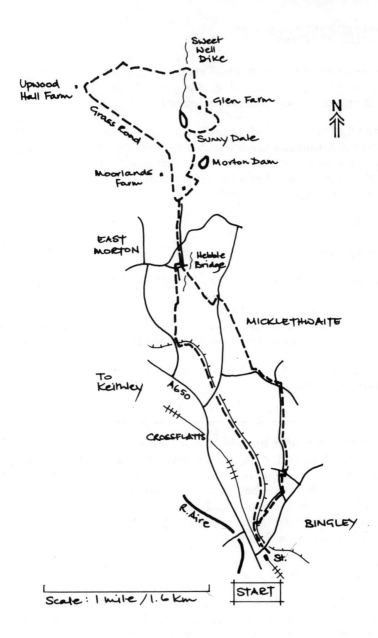

raise the canal 60 feet and each lock measures 62 feet by 14 feet and 4 inches. They were considered one of the wonders of the canal age when they were built and are still are a remarkable feat, a model of them still to be seen in the Science Museum in South Kensington.

Five Rise Locks, Bingley

Continue past both staircases and along the canal towpath between the canal and house gardens, soon passing above Crossflatts and crossing the road to Micklethwaite. At the next road and bridge across the canal, by Lingcroft Wharf, cross the canal to walk along Moreton Lane but almost immediately take a gap stile down steps leading to a narrow enclosed footpath across a field, soon bearing left into woods and climbing behind gardens to another stile.

This contours around a grassy hillside with views across Morton Beck to Micklethwaite before descending to a stile by a gate into a short cul-de-sac lane, Hawthorne Way. At the junction turn right into another descending lane. On the left, almost opposite the road sign for Cliffe Mill

Fold, are a couple of converted farmhouses whose cobbled drive is a
public path, marked by lamp posts. Follow this enclosed lane past yet
another converted barn and farm to emerge at a cobbled yard at East
Morton on the main Otley Road.

Cross, and bear slightly left to stone steps which lead into Greenend
Road. Walk along this long street past cottages, a Methodist Chapel and
a graveyard. There are intriguing views down into the valley on the
right. Ignore tracks bearing off left and right, passing Sunnydale Park
and Morton Hall, but as you reach Boany Hall, with its pillared gateway,
take the narrow path to the left over a stile. Alongside a field wall to
another stile, bear right to join a track which contours round the hillside,
soon bearing right through a gateway and into woods. Ahead is a
reservoir dam which once supplied waterpower for the mills of this
valley, Sunnydale. Sunnydale Mill whose remains can still be glimpsed
through the trees, had one of the largest waterwheels in the British Isles,
fed by a massive mill race or goit.

You can walk up to the reservoir embankment to overlook the little
artificial lake with its reflecting trees, and rejoin the main track below the
dam by a steeply stepped path, or retrace your steps and cross by the
bridge. The main track now circles round below the dam and ascends
woods above Sunnydale, emerging at a gateway. Follow the track
through fields, soon joining a wallside and curving to the left towards
Glen Farm.

Sweet Well Dike

About 50 metres before the farm take the field gate right, and cross the
field behind along a fainter grassy way to another gate ahead. Bear left
to a third gate, then swing right to yet another gate by a curious little
stone barn. The track now serpentines once again to the left through a
gate and bridge over Sweet Well Dike, and another gate in the field
corner. Continue alongside the wall on the right towards top corner of
the woods ahead, where the track dips past the Glen and ascends along
a wall to Upwood Farm ahead.

As you approach the farmyard, go through the gate on the left which
leads into a muddy track alongside the fence to a gate where this
becomes an enclosed farm track. However, where it swings left into a

field, go through the cattle gate ahead into a lovely, typical Pennine, green track with the name Grass Road. Grass Road dips gently down towards East Morton, bearing left and steeply into a stone way before joining the track from Moorlands Farm and rejoining Greenend Road.

Holroyd Mill

Retrace your steps along Greenend Road back to the Otley Road, crossing to locate the path by the converted barns, but when your reach Cliffe Mill Fold do not turn left, but go right where you'll find, on the right, a narrow waymarked path which twists down behind cottages to a footbridge Hebble Bridge (the name suggesting it replaced stepping stones) over Morton Beck. Follow it uphill as it becomes a lovely old cobbled packhorse way climbing up to Micklethwaite, where it emerges by cottages, Holroyd Mill (now a Craft Centre) and Spring well Farm.

Micklethwaite is all that its name suggests, a linear village crammed with weavers' cottages and fine old Jacobean yeoman's houses, all black gritstone, narrow windows and steep gables. It's worth turning left for a hundred metres or so just to enjoy them. The Manor House on the left with a date stone 1601 predates even these.

Otherwise turn right up the steep village street to the top green to where the road hairpins sharply left. Your way is through the pedestrian gate, right, immediately below the drive to the Bungalow. Follow the faint path across the field ahead towards Fairlady Farm ahead, through a gate and stile. Beyond this you will find another of those delectable packhorse paths, once no doubt used by travelling piecemen or merchants collecting cloth by pony between farms. This path goes through a little gate and contours below a steep hillside before emerging at yet another old farm and the road from Crossflatts. Turn left up the hill past ivy covered walls and grand houses of Greenhill Lane to the junction. Keep right, but almost immediately go right through a metal kissing gate. This leads to a fieldside path which descends to another kissing gate and cross a track to join yet another enclosed lane, all stone walls and rhododendrons, behind gardens.

Keep the same direction through a squeezer stile at the next crossing road. Keep ahead on a new-ish estate road, Pinelands, to the left of whose last house the path continues again past gardens. Keep in the same direction at crossroads until the path eventually joins a driveway leading into Beck Lane, opposite a large Edwardian House. Cross to Hall Beck Drive, continuing past a variety of houses and the British Legion before taking the second road right, Plevna Terrace, an unsurfaced street, towards the old mill ahead. Make for the right of the mill to a track by the canalside. Turn left along the canal to Three Rise Locks again, crossing at the footbridge between the locks. Turn left, but opposite the central locks look for a narrow path on the right between stone walls and allotments, marked by a lamp post, which zigzags under the railway to emerge in Bingley's busy main street opposite the town's handsome Tudor century church.

Bingley

Bingley is a medieval town which enjoyed a new lease of life in the Industrial Revolution brought by the canal era. It richly repays exploration: the old stocks and Market Cross are in Myrtle Park, and the town has many fascinating corners. The Old Queen's Head on the left hand side of Main Street towards the railway station is an unpretentious 1930s pub, with a choice of excellent guest beers in additional to the resident ale, a pleasant atmosphere and good food. It's only three minutes' walk from the station. If you cross the bridge in Park Road and go down the steps towards the canalside, which leads to the Leeds platform and the car park, you'll notice the proud letters MR – Midland Railway – carved in the stone of the totally unnecessary street-facing archway. Victorian extravagance, but what splendid exuberance.

24. OTLEY CHEVIN

A walk of contrasts – riverside, parkland and woodland, and a favourite West Yorkshire viewpoint in the lower Dales.

Pub: The Half Moon, Pool-in-Wharfedale. Younger's Scotch Bitter and No 3, Tetley Bitter, Theakston's Bitter. Open: Monday to Saturday 1130 – 1500 and 1730 – 2300; Sunday 1200 – 1500 and 1900 – 2230. Food available lunchtime and evening.

Start: The Old Bridge, Otley

Distance: 7 miles (12 km)

Maps: Pathfinder Sheet 672; Landranger Sheet 104 Leeds & Bradford.

Public Transport: Yorkshire Rider 780,784 from Leeds; 653/654 from Bradford/Harrogate. Metro Day Rover tickets valid.

By Car: Wide choice of car parks in Otley

Otley is a fine old Dales market and coaching town with a medieval heart of narrow lanes and courtyards, a cobbled marketplace, many 18th and 19th century houses, old mills, inns and workshops and an impressive main fifteenth century church. There are links with Thomas Chippendale, the famous furniture maker born in the town in 1718. The town is overlooked by the massive green ridge of Otley Chevin, now a Forest Park, and the destination of this walk.

Ancient Bridge

Start from the ancient seven-arched bridge over the River Wharfe, easily reached from car parks or bus station along the Pateley road. Cross the river, turning sharp right once over the bridge, and down steps to the riverside gardens with its pleasant café (open in winter). Keep on the riverside, past the footbridge where the tarmac ends and along a narrow riverside path (an ancient road not marked as a right of way on the OS map) which soon leaves the town and goes through open countryside on the edge of Farnley Parkland past the gravel ponds of Knotford Nook.

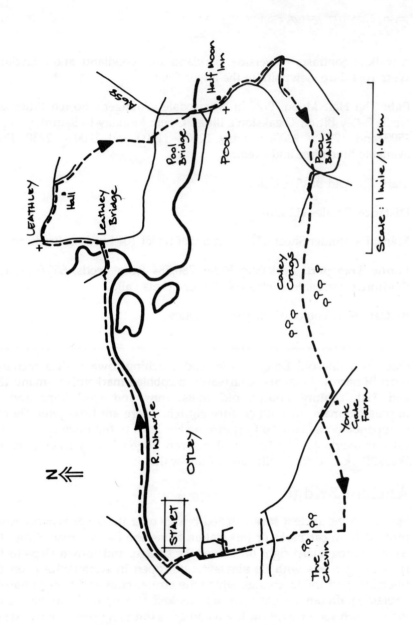

The path eventually bears left over the field to a stile in the Leathley-Farnley road. Turn right to cross the bridge and Leathley Lodge to the dangerously busy road to Killinghall. Turn left here. Keep on the narrow grassy verge to the village of Leathley whose fine church has a rare Anglo-Norman tower, mounting block, stocks. Nearby stands a row of fine 18th century almshouses.

Leathley Hall

Your way continues along the lane to Stainburn on the right, but almost immediately you leave the main road, keep ahead as the lane bears left along what appears to be the tarmac entrance to Leathley Hall but is an old public road. Follow this narrow lane past Leathley Hall to where, behind the Hall gardens, a path with a green metal sign leads along a grassy track to a stile. Cross here, following the fence on the left through parkland. As the fence bears right, go through the stile by the gate on the left, keeping to the opposite side of the same fence down to a slightly awkward double stile at the bottom of the field, the path now on the left side of the hedge down to the main road. Cross, the way continuing over another stile slightly to the left which leads to Pool Bridge over the Wharfe. Cross to the safety of the pavement on the far side of the bridge.

There is now some unavoidable road walking on the A658 accompanied by heavy traffic through the centre of Pool (keep on the left hand side) until, opposite the church, you reach the haven of the Half Moon Inn in a row of cottages. This pleasant pub offers a variety of real ales including the excellent Younger's Number 3 and a choice of good food.

Continue from the pub up the hill on the main Bradford road past the junction with the A659 Harewood road, and Old Pool Bank on the right. Keep ahead as you begin to climb up Pool Bank, but just before the road veers right, cross to go under a stone arch inscribed "Avenue des Hirondelles" – the Avenue of the Swallows. Follow a broad stony track underneath an avenue of fine horsechestnut trees. The arch and lane are a surviving portion of an Edwardian development which did not come fully to fruition. Climb up the hill until the track peters out at a stile. Keep ahead, but where the now grassy chestnut avenue comes to a dead end, bear slightly right to a stile in the wood ahead.

Pool Bank

You are now in an old quarry, completely covered in trees. Take the path which curves up a steep slope to the left. Keep straight on to where the path levels out past cottages on Pool Bank, going back into the wood before joining the drive and the main Leeds road (A660) at Pool Bar, a former turnpike tollbooth.

Cross the busy road with care, turning right for about 200 metres downhill to where a drive and steps bear off left. Your way is the lower path, a tarmac drive and private road (public path) past a stone house. Keep ahead where the drive ends to follow a flagged path which leads through the heather and behind the gritstone outcrops Caley Crags, maintaining the same direction into the Danefield Estate, now part of the Chevin Forest Park. From here are magnificent, panoramic views across Wharfedale and Washburndale, the tributary valley of the Wharfe.

Keep ahead through the woodland, the path dipping to a footbridge and emerging at a car park below York Gate Farm. Turn right at the road and walk downhill for 300 metres, taking the second of two paths left, signed West Chevin, which is a sandy track climbing to a stile and wallside path to the summit of The Chevin. Keep ahead past the car park to the summit crag, just before which is a viewfinder indicating items that can be seen in the distance on both sides of the long ridge. The name "Chevin" is reputedly Celtic in origin, referring to a hillside.

White House

Retrace your steps for 100 metres before forking left down a sandy path which descends through the woods and over a series of steps down the hillside. To the left is The White House Visitor Centre with a Tea House (cafeteria) which is open most days in summer and on Sundays in winter. The path continues down cobbled steps, over a footbridge across the by-pass and former railway station (much lamented) past a long row of terraces houses into the centre of Otley, emerging by the church. Turn right along Bondgate for the bus station.

If you proceed a little farther along Bondgate, you'll reach The Junction, an excellent real ale pub with a good choice of beers, a roaring fire (in winter) and plenty of atmosphere.

25. WINDGATE NICK AND ADDINGHAM

From the 'Heather Spa' of Ilkley to the old mill village of Addingham in Wharfedale, with high level views across the Yorkshire Dales.

Pub: The Fleece, Addingham. Tetley's Bitter and Mild. Open Monday to Saturday 1130 – 1500 and 1800 – 2300; Sunday 1200 – 1600. Food daily 1200 – 1400; evenings 1900 – 2100.

Start: Ilkley Station

Distance: 8 miles (14 km)

Map: Pathfinder Sheet 671; Landranger Sheet 104 Leeds and Bradford.

Public Transport: Frequent Metro Train Wharfedale Line services from Leeds and Bradford Forster Square (Sundays included) (BR Table 37); Bus 733, 784 from Leeds, 650, 651 from Bradford, 762,765 from Keighley. Metro Day Rover valid.

By Car: Large car park in the centre of Ilkley (signed off Brook Street).

Ilkley was originally a Celtic settlement and a small fort called *Olicana*. It was established by occupying Romans in the First Century AD at an important fording point across the River Wharfe. It remained a quiet Dales village community over the ensuing centuries with little more than an ancient church, village school and scatter of cottages around a stream. This changed in the late 18th and early 19th centuries when its fame grew as a moorland 'hydropathic' spa town – the 'Heather Spa' – with several hotels where guests took cold water cures and enjoyed brisk walks on the famous heather moors. It later became a commuter retreat for wealthy Bradford wool merchants, but still keeps much of its former elegance, a popular area for shopping, coffee drinking, walking and sightseeing.

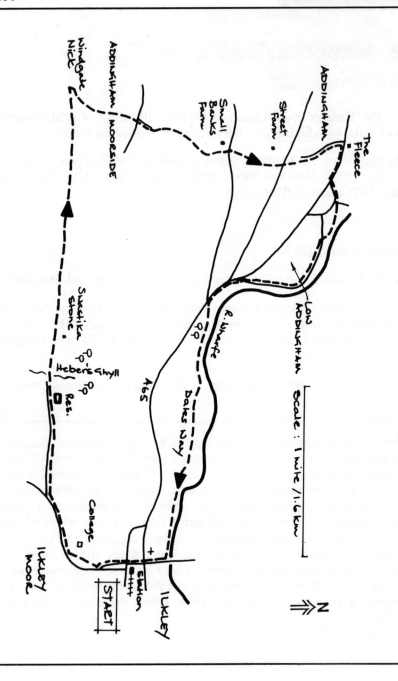

Wells Promenade

From the Station piazza, cross Station Road at the zebra crossing, and make your way to Wells Promenade, opposite the traffic island, where you'll find a path that winds its way up narrow gardens by a stream. Follow it uphill to the gate at the top, crossing the road to continue on the unsurfaced road ahead past new flats. At the end of this road is a gateway. Go through it and cross in front of lodge gates to a wooden kissing gate leading to an enclosed path on the right that continues to follow the stream uphill. This emerges opposite Ilkley Moor.

Springtime in Ilkley

Famous Common

Thanks to a Victorian popular song which now enjoys the status of a folk song: "On Ilkla moor Baht 'At", this wild expanse of heather moor, bilberry and bracken is perhaps Britain's most famous common, a place for thousands of West Riding people to take air and exercise.

Follow the road along the edge of the as it curves past the edge of the Moor, past Ilkley College, the former Hydro designed by Cuthbert Broderick, architect of Leeds Town Hall. Where the road comes out at a junction, take the narrower road left and uphill. After about 300 metres, above the houses look for and branch off right along a path which crosses a beck by an ornamental moorland track. This then becomes a track above house gardens along the edge of the moor.

Heber's Ghyll

Follow this along past a reservoir, gradually gaining height, before dipping over another ornamental bridge and through a kissing gate entering a steep wooded valley, Heber's Ghyll. Ignore steps going downhill to more bridges, but make for the path to the right of the shelter which leads to another kissing gate onto the moor. Follow the path to right as it winds through bracken, soon branching left on a narrow way to join a broader track.

Swastika Stone

Now bear right towards a curious boulder surrounded by a fence you'll see on the moor edge. This is the celebrated Swastika Stone, a carved rock probably of late Bronze Age or early Iron Age in origin. The original carving, now faint, has been replicated with a modern carving easier to see, the "Swastika" design nothing to do with the Third Reich but an ancient "folyfoot" being a prehistoric, Indo-European symbol of eternal life.

This is also a magnificent viewpoint, looking across to Beamsley Beacon and the great sweep of Wharfedale towards Bolton Abbey and Simon Seat, with Cookrise Crag to the west.

Windgate Nick

The path continues along the moor edge, over two closely positioned stiles across a narrow field, and then a series of stiles, with the moor falling steeply away to the right past crags, and rough grazing to the left. Continue for just over a mile, until the path finally begins to level out in an expanse of open heather, and you begin to see over the crest of the moor into Airedale to the south. Now at the point where you find yourself almost directly opposite a gap stile in the wall in the moor to the left, your way is right, swinging down a deep natural cleft in the crags. This is Windgate nick, "gate" meaning road.

Make your way carefully down to the bottom of the nick across a boulder field, partially create by quarrying the millstone grit. Look out for a magnificent millstone propped up to your left.

Just past this stone, your way is to the right, below the boulder field, along an extremely faint path. Now look to the crossing wall that slopes down from the moorland crags ahead, and make your way, still over the open moor, to a rickety stile in the centre of that wall.

Cross, and walk down a long field, heading not to the first wall corner, but following the left hand wall across a slightly boggy area as it curves round to a lower corner where concealed from view there is a stonestile. Cross, still following the wall down, now on your right, across a beck and stile to meet the lane at Addingham Moorside.

Your way is along the track almost directly ahead, a private drive. Where it swings right, bear left along the signposted path which dips down a grassy slope. Look for the stile in the wall directly ahead, keeping the same direction across a pasture to another stile, and then bear right down to a stream where you'll find a little footbridge. Cross, keeping ahead in the same direction but climbing steeply uphill. As you approach the barn ahead at Small Banks Farm, look for the stile in the wall by the barn corner, leading to the lane by a telephone kiosk.

The path, signposted, lies directly ahead over a stile and alongside the fence, keeping ahead and slightly left to another stile and then alongside the fence to a little of footbridge over another beck. The path keeps alongside the fence, up steps to emerge by Street Farm and a broad field where once ran a Roman Road, hence the name Street Farm. Keep almost the same direction now towards the new Addingham by-pass which at this point lies in a deep cutting. To the left you'll see new signposts and stiles, and crossing point. Cross with care, as traffic speeds are high and visibility not always good. The path emerges into a narrow lane, Stockinger Lane.

Stockinger Lane

Stockinger Lane lies between some attractive old buildings in this remarkable Dales mill village, whose water powered and riverside mills are mostly converted to houses or warehouses. They were amongst the earliest of the Industrial Revolution, but many fine cottages, workshops and tall houses of the period remain.

The lane comes out at The Fleece, a fine early 19th century coaching inn. Its original stables for the changing of stagecoach horses before they ascended Chelker Brow towards Skipton. There is beautifully kept Tetley Bitter and Mild on offer, a choice of good pub grub from the simple to the sophisticated, and on winter days a friendly fire – as well as excellent Trad Jazz on Wednesday evenings.

If you've had enough at this point, Buses 748, 762 (Sundays) or 765 will take you back to Ilkley. Otherwise turn left outside the pub, and walk along Main Street, mercifully freed from the ceaseless roar of A65 traffic now filling the by-pass. Where the road branches, bear left along Church Lane to its junction with North Street, the main Bolton Abbey road. Cross to the footpath and no parking sign on the left, to cross a tiny footbridge leading to Addingham's impressive medieval church. The path follows the outside of the churchyard wall, before turning right alongside the hedge and crossing a little hump backed bridge to the lane. Turn right past old and new Rectories, to the end of the cul-de-sac and over the stile into Low Addingham. There used to be a large woollen mill with attendant millworkers' cottages, but is now a Civic Trust Award winning development with early Industrial Revolution cottages of the turn of the last century turned to bijou homes.

Dales Way

Walk straight through the village, and along the riverside sidewalk to eventually join the old Addingham road, now a quiet lane. Turn left here for some 300 metres to where the lane swings right. Your way – part of the 81 mile Dales Way between Ilkley and Bowness-on-Windermere – lies straight ahead below woods, soon cutting across a riverside pasture. Keep ahead across a rather boggy stream, to a more elevated riverside path over a footbridge and past house gardens before opening out again into pasture. The path leaves the riverside alongside a fence, keeping ahead through well marked kissing gates to join the drive to Ilkley Sports Centre.

Keep right here, but where the drive swings uphill to the A65, keep ahead along the narrower riverside track to Ilkley Bridge, the lovely old 17th century arched stone bridge over the Wharfe. This is closed to traffic and is the official start of the Dales Way. Timothy Taylor afficianados might like to note that the Vaults, about 50 metres uphill from the Bridge, sells Taylor's Best Bitter and Landlord, and Tetleys' Bitter and Mild.

Riverside Gardens

The path continues past riverside gardens, (Sam Smiths available at the Riverside pub with its riverside beer garden) boating and recreational areas to the road bridge over the river. Turn right past the site of Ilkley's Roman fort and its medieval church (with superb Anglo-Viking churchyard crosses now kept safely inside) to the traffic lights. Ahead to bus and railway station, car park and Ilkley's shops, cafés and yet more pubs.

26. LOTHERSDALE

A short but fairly strenuous walk which has almost every typical features of the Pennines and explores a little known and unspoiled mill village and dale.

Pub: The Hare and Hounds, Lothersdale. Webster's Pennine Bitter and Green Label, Tetley Bitter, Wilson's Mild. Open: Monday to Saturday 1200 – 1500 and 1900 – 2300. Food available 1200 – 1400 and 1900 – 2130.

Start: Cononley.

Distance: 7 miles (10 km)

Map: Pathfinder 670; Landranger 103 Blackburn.

Public Transport: Frequent service from Leeds/Bradford Forster Sq. (Sundays inclusive) to Cononley on Airedale line (BR Table 36). Metro Day Rover valid to Steeton and Silsden – pay excess to Cononley.

By Car: Park in Cononley.

Cononley is a small, compact mill village tucked into the side of high moorland at the northern end of Airedale, and close to old lead mine workings. Its large mill survives, though now devoted to light engineering, whilst several of the millworkers cottages and old farms have now become sought after commuter homes.

From Cononley Station turn left along the road from the station and level crossing, past the Railway Inn, with a brook and playground on the left. Immediately past the Methodist Church turn sharp right into Moorfoot Lane. Just past the bridge over the railway, take the farm track left where you'll see a narrow gap stile by the gate indicating the line of a path alongside the railway and into the adjacent field.

Cross to and follow the railway embankment, but at the ladder stile and warning sign where another path joins from the left, bear right where you will see two gateways. Yours is the opening on the right, leading into a long, narrow field at the far right hand corner of which there is a narrow pedestrian gate leading into another farm track, Shady Lane.

River Aire

Follow this track right as it leads to the side of the River Aire. It eventually peters out, leaving you walking along a grassy flood embankment above the river. Head through a pedestrian gate towards a concrete sewage outflow where you turn sharp left to locate a faint green

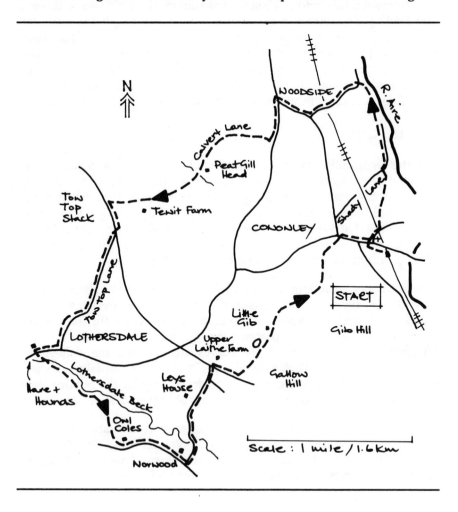

track leading back across the open field towards the hamlet of Cononley Woodside to your left. The track bends left towards a fieldgate leading into an enclosed track by holly trees. Keep ahead as it passes and joins the drive of a very much rebuilt farmhouse and leads into the lane at Woodside.

Turn right here and climb up the steep lane, eventually reaching a cross roads where you turn sharp left, the ascent now getting even steeper. The lane curves up to the right, but there are fine views along the valley to compensate. Just before the steep hill sign on the right, you will see a gate leading to a concrete track to a barn. Go through the gate, but immediately leave the track to go sharply right along the wallside along an ancient bridleway which soon becomes a partially enclosed grassy track, Calvert Lane. At the next gate the way is to the left of an old, almost vanished wall. Keep straight ahead as you cross an open field, making for a bridlegate and the farm ahead known as Peat Gill Head.

Tewit Farm

Pass the farm buildings on the right hand side to join a crossing lane. Keep right here along a deep sunken, narrow farm track, gently climbing uphill through gates, with the wall on your right. This climbs more steeply and bears right to reach a gate onto the open moor, with Tewit Farm to the left. Tewit is dialect for Lapwing, though skylarks are perhaps more common. Follow the track fainter now through heather until you reach the lane from Carleton at Tow Top Slack.

Turn left here and follow the lane for some 200 metres to where a clear track forks to the right. Take this track, Tow Top Lane, over the brow of Tow Top hill before it descends into Lothersdale. Where the track bends sharp right to the farm keep ahead through the gate and onto a lovely old green lane which suddenly curves steeply into the valley, the chimney of Wilson's Mill directly ahead. Cross an old, partially quarried, grassy area heading for the narrow, enclosed way in the bottom right hand corner which brings you out into east of Lothersdale at Dale End.

Turn right downhill to the Hare and House, a comfortable traditional tavern close to the mill. There's good ale – Webster's and Tetley's and a choice of food on offer, though with such clean carpets the landlord appreciates walkers' boots and rucksacks being left outside.

Lothersdale

Lothersdale is a long, narrow village squeezing into its valley which has somehow avoided yuppification, remaining very much a working village. Wilson's Mill, with its fine chimney and cluster of cottages reinforces that character. If you notice quite a few bed and breakfast signs, it's because the Pennine Way runs through the village and crosses our route in the village.

The route continues past the mill. Cross to the mill yard, and make your way to the left past the cottages and manager's house. Head towards the chimney, to the left of which there is a gate leading to a track by the stream, Lothersdale Beck.

Follow this track, through another gate and along a charming, shallow valley, partially wooded. Where it opens out into as a broader stream. Ignore the footbridge on the left and keep straight ahead, parallel with the stream across a slightly marshy area of ground, making for a little footbridge you'll see ahead, behind which is a stile. Cross both, but now leave the streamside to climb the hillock on the right, towards the hedge and wall. At the top right hand corner of the field, a gate and stile leads into an enclosed track to a farm, Owl Cotes, on a narrow lane.

Low Lane

Keep left along this deep sunken lane, Low Lane, soon passing an old farm, Norwood, not far beyond which an old green track Benton Gap Lane crosses Low Lane. Turn left here and follow this lovely old way as it winds steeply down to the stream. Cross the stream by a footbridge and ascend steeply up the other side. You pass Ley's House and join the farm track to the lane. Bear left as this lane swings to a junction at Upper Laithe Farm, where you turn right for some 200 metres to where a footpath marked by a green sign indicates a path over a stile.

Ahead are the remains of old lead mine workings with a smelt mill chimney on the summit of Gib Hill, and the ominously named Gallows Hill to the right. This was once an important area for lead with rich seams of galena, lead ore, on the edge of the limestone which runs across from Lothersdale. The proximity of Gallows Hill suggests the lawless state of early mining communities.

The path cuts across to a stile in the fence ahead before bearing to the right hand side of the pond and two more stile in fences. Head for the nearest of two farms, Little Gib, opposite which is a stone step stile leading to the farm track. Keep ahead past Little Gib and through the gate along the track leading to the left hand side of Great Gib (ignore the path branching off right). The next gate ahead leads into a green track which soon contours around the hillside giving magnificent views across Cononley village.

This track eventually dips down sharply, views extending across the whole Aire Gap, before reaching a gate which leads to a steep lane which drops steeply into the topside of Cononley village. Turn right into Main Street, keeping left at the junction to Cononley Station.

27. LANGBER LANE

A ramble along a fine old pre-turnpike highway in Ribblesdale

Pub: The Golden Lion, Settle. Thwaite's Bitter. Open Monday to Saturday 1130 – 1500 and 1800 – 2300; Sunday 1200 – 1500 and 1900 – 2230.

Start: Long Preston

Distance: 5 miles (8 km).

Map: Outdoor Leisure, Sheet 10 Yorkshire Dales Southern area; Landranger Sheets 98, 103.

Public Transport: Long Preston Station on the Leeds-Carnforth line (not winter Sundays) – return from Settle. Book Settle Day Return (BR Table 36). Pennine Motors Skipton-Ingleton service provides regular bus services Skipton-Long Preston-settle, including Sundays.

By Car: Park Long Preston Station and return by Pennine bus or rail service from Giggleswick (1.5 miles from Settle); note most trains from Settle station do not stop at Long Preston. Alternatively return to Long Preston via Mitchell Lane and Hunter Bark (4 miles) – see below.

From Long Preston Station walk towards the village, taking the narrow, enclosed footpath (signed) on the left before the first houses which leads behind the village past cottages. This emerges at a stile opposite the lower Green. Turn right and then first left into the main Village Green, crossing the A65 to the War Memorial and Maypole.

Walk straight ahead past the Green and into School Lane, a narrow road almost directly opposite. At the village school where the lane bends right, take the fork left along a narrow farm track, Scalehaw Lane. As this passes the farm, Hewit House, it becomes a green way, widening and descending to Long Preston Beck, which is crossed by a footbridge.

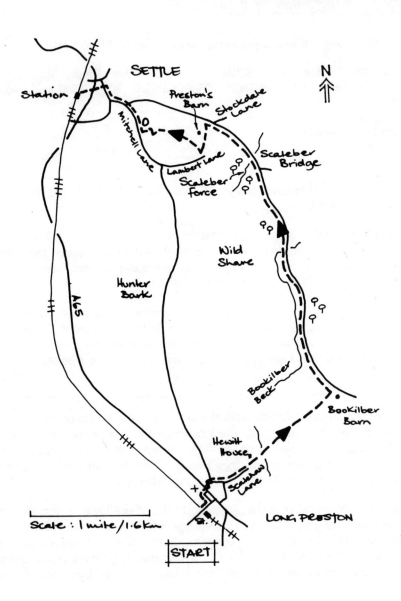

SETTLE

Station

Preston's Barn

Stockdale Lane

Mitchell Lane

Lambert Lane

Scaleber Bridge

Scaleber Force

Wild Share

Hunter Bark

A65

Bookilber Beck

Bookilber Barn

Hewitt House

Scaleber Lane

LONG PRESTON

Scale : 1 mile/1·6 km

START

N

Your route, signed to Langber Lane, is half left, up a grassy bank and to the right of a small circular reservoir enclosed by a stone wall topped by protective wire. Look for the waymark on the wall.

The path crosses to and follows the wall up Scalehaw Hill to a gap stile ahead. Cross, and you will see two ladder stiles marking the path ahead. The first is just ahead and to the right, but the second is reached after a steady climb across a wide field. Your efforts are more than compensated by superb views behind across Ribblesdale to Pendle Hill and the West Pennine Moors beyond.

At the second ladder stile your way is indicated by the roof of Bookilber Barn, a farm, ahead. Make for the stile and kissing gate in the wall ahead and then descend a shallow ravine before climbing back towards Bookilber. Two ladder stiles to the left of the farm lead into Langber Lane. Turn left here.

Langber Lane

Langber Lane is an ancient cross Pennine highway which was in use long before the main Keighley-Kendal turnpike road, now the A65, was constructed in the 18th century. It was the old Leeds to Kendal road, and once carried substantial traffic by horse, pack pony, and cart between what were already important centres of the textile trade in the 17th century. It remains as an ancient road, still easy traceable as it runs between enclosure walls as a track, minor road or footpath between Skipton and Settle via Gargrave, Bell Busk, Otterburn and Bookilber.

It is partially surfaced west of Bookilber and provides easy, relaxed walking, gently curving northwards as it winds its way along a shallow ravine formed by Bookilber Beck. You pass Bookilber Plantation on the right, with its handsome pines, and soon reach a larger coniferous woodland, Wild Share, on the left.

As you reach the summit of the road, magnificent panoramic views of the shattered limestone cliffs of Upper Ribblesdale open out before you like miniature Dolomites. The spectacular formations directly ahead are Warrendale Knotts with the massive expanse of Attermire Scar to the right. If there is any sunlight, the light-reflecting rock gleams white against the soft greens of the pastures.

Scalebar Bridge

At the road junction with the Airton road, keep ahead down to Scalebar Bridge. Just past the Bridge a ladder stile gives access to the little wood and if you keep to the clear top path (other routes are dangerous) you can walk round to the far side of the wooded gorge to enjoy a superb view of Scalebar Force, an impressive waterfall, particularly after any recent rain.

Return to the Airton road by the nearer stile, both gap and ladder stile are on offer. Walk along the lane in the Settle direction for about 400 metres, past the junction with Stockdale Lane and the bridlepath to Malham, to where a green track, Lambert Lane, runs between stone walls past a fine old barn known as Preston's Barn.

Follow Lambert Lane to where it bears right and then some 80 metres from the corner go through the gate, right, signposted to Settle. Follow the wall on the right along a faint grassy path. This soon bears left. Keep the wall on your right as you reach and cross a somewhat awkward stone gap and step stile in a crossing wall. Continue alongside the wall as it curves to the right to reach a ladder stile in the corner of the large enclosure. Cross to see another gap stile in a fragment of wall ahead.

Mitchell Lane

Turn sharp right beyond this wall, heading for an enclosed small reservoir and wood. The path descends alongside this wall (most people will zigzag down the hillside to ease the steepness of the gradient) to a gate in the fence in the bottom corner. This leads to a track below the reservoir and a metal gate into Mitchell Lane. Keep right here towards Settle.

Motorists returning from Settle wanting to get back to Long Preston could follow the way left over Hunter's Bark. It is asphalted for much of the way, apart from a central rocky section but is easy to follow and without traffic.

Settle

Otherwise, the route to Settle is downhill to where Mitchell Lane meets the Airton Road with views across Settle and Giggleswick against a background of magnificent hill scenery: the Yorkshire Dales to the North and the Bowland Fells to the South, Ribblesdale in between. The green copper dome of Giggleswick School chapel is a notable landmark. You soon reach cobbled Victoria Street in Upper Settle, and pass the curious Folly, a magnificent 17th century town house. You emerge in Settle marketplace by the Town Hall, and the unique Shambles with their twin storeys of shops topped by dwellings.

Settle is one of the loveliest towns in the Yorkshire Dales. It is rich in fascinating architecture, much of it dating from the 17th and 18th centuries. There are old courts and warehouses, cottages, fine Georgian town houses, interesting shops, and, if you have time, Castlebergh Rock – an impressive limestone crag and viewpoint, reached from the road behind the Trustees Savings Bank. Go through a gateway on the right and follow the zigzagging path uphill.

The Golden Lion in Duke Street (the main street towards the station) has a datestone 1671 over its side doorway, but was almost certainly expanded into a large coaching inn in the early 19th century to deal with the thriving Leeds-Lancaster/Kendal stagecoach trade. It has kept much of its old coaching in atmosphere with big rooms, a large yard at the back once used for stabling horses (now a garage) and in the main bar, a roaring wood fire. The draught Thwaite's Bitter is delicious and a choice of good food is available at most times.

Even if you don't return from Settle Station, it is worth having a look at what is probably (with Appleby) one of the finest examples in the North of a small country station still in use. Built by the Midland Railway in 1876 on the Settle-Carlisle line in a standard Midland style known affectionately as "Derby Gothic", it has such long forgotten country station luxuries as proper waiting room with information, loos that work, and a ticket office with helpful and well informed staff – at most times.

28. CRUMMACKDALE

A walk through classic limestone country to take advantage of two scenic railways in the Yorkshire Dales, the celebrated Settle-Carlisle and the much neglected Skipton-Lancaster line, and to visit a popular real ale pub.

Pub: The New Inn, Clapham. Dent Bitter, Tetleys Bitter, Younger's No 3, McEwans 80 Shilling, plus guest beer in summer (usually Moorhouses); Open Monday to Saturday 1130 – 1530ish and 1900 – 2300; Sunday 1200 – 1500 and 1900 – 2230. Food: morning coffee; breakfast; lunch 1200 – 1400; dinner 1900 – 2100.

Distance: 7 miles (11 km)

Maps: Ordnance Survey Outdoor Leisure Sheet 2, Yorkshire Dales Western Area.

Public Transport: Outwards catch the Leeds-Settle-Carlisle train to Horton-in-Ribblesdale, book Horton Day Return, return from Clapham on Lancaster line (both BR Table 36). Tickets are usually valid to return from both stations or with only a small excess payable.

By Car: Park either at Skipton or Settle Station and book Horton-in-Ribblesdale Day Return. If returning to Settle catch the train from Clapham and alight at Giggleswick and walk to Settle (1^1/$_2$ miles).

From Horton Station go through the pedestrian gate at the Settle end of the platform, continuing to the stile ahead. The path, part of the Three Peaks Walk, bears right across pasture climbing slightly over a knoll before descending towards Beecroft Hall Farm. Keep right past the farm to a gap where the path, well defined and generally busy with mud bespattered walkers from Ingleborough, bears left and begins to ascend steeply past limestone outcrops, with increasingly fine views back across Horton and across Ribblesdale with the magnificent profile of Pen-y-Ghent as a backcloth behind.

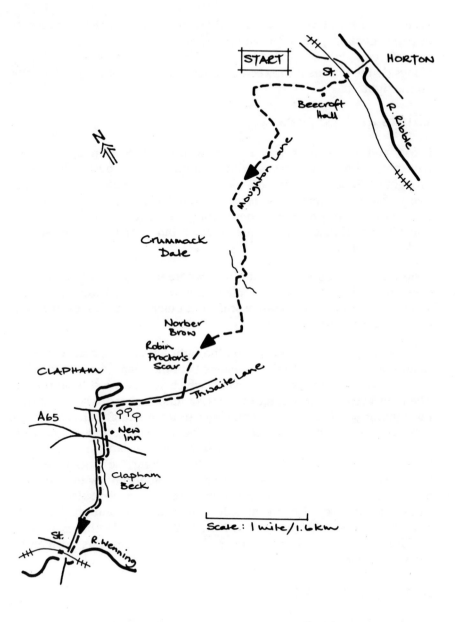

Where the ascent levels onto a broad grassy shelf you reach a cross road of paths. Look to your left where in the wall corner about 400 metres on the left you will see a ladder stile. Head for this, cross and keep alongside the wall as it dips across rough pasture to another ladder stile on the right.

Clints and Grykes

Cross, and make your way over a spectacular plateau of limestone pavement, clints and grykes with scattered juniper bushes known as Moughton. Take great care on the slippery rock, heading in a straight line where, by a cairn, you reach a natural nick on the plateau. This leads to a lovely green path descending past between limestone scars into Crummackdale, one of the remoter but grander of the smaller Yorkshire Dales.

Follow the path down to a gate from where it becomes a fine enclosed green track, Moughton Lane. Follow this track as it bends left in the valley bottom under impressive scars and outcrops not just of limestone but of ancient Silurian slates.

You eventually reach a junction on the right with a ford and twin stone footbridges. Cross, and take the stone-bottomed lane which ascends a gigantic boulder, immediately beyond which you take a stile on the left. The path goes to the summit of a grassy hillock ahead where just over the summit you'll see the next stile ahead. Keep straight ahead to more stiles across a farm track before bearing right to join the lane from Crummackdale at a stile. Immediately across the lane, a second stile leads to a superb footpath which contours along the edge of Norber Brow past an area of rare geological unconformity with the huge limestone outcrop of Nappa Scar lying directly on ancient slates. A stile leads to a path ascending the hillside behind this scar onto the limestone pavement above with the famous Norber Erratics, huge lichen covered boulders of Silurian Slate carried to their often precarious position by ancient glaciers.

Robin Proctor's Scar

A tall footpath sign below the main slope and bulk of Robin Proctor's Scar indicates the line of path across a ladder stile and alongside a curving wall. As the wall swings left, your path crosses open, rough pasture with the sunken remains of an ancient tarn, still marked by walls, to the right. Head directly across the pasture to a ladder stile into Thwaite Lane, an old unsurfaced lane which leads into Clapham Village under a couple of unusual and fascinating tunnels, built to keep travellers outside the Ingleborough Hall Estate.

Clapham

Clapham is one of the most delightful villages of the Yorkshire Dales. It occupies the bottom end of a valley that drains off the shoulder of Ingleborough mountain, its twin streets running along each side of a stream crossed by bridges. If you've time, combine this walk with a visit to Ingleborough Cave, via the Reginald Farrer Trail through the Ingleborough Hall Estate, reached through the woodyard at top of the village. There is also an unusual Regency Church, a choice of cafés, loos, a post office and shop, the Dalesman magazine's offices and the National Park Centre in the old Manor House with a good range of literature and some interesting displays.

The New Inn at the bottom of the village, by the old main road bridge, is a fine old coaching inn, dating from 1776 and the great days of stage coaches along the busy Keighley-Kendal turnpike. You're more likely to find cavers and walkers in the pub than stagecoachmen nowadays, tempting by the good selection of real ales, including the locally brewed Dent Bitter, and plenty of food. If you decide to stay a little longer, the pub has a choice of en suite rooms on offer and will even arrange a guided walk for you.

Give yourself ample time, about half an hour, to cover the $1^1/_4$ miles to Clapham Station; the unsurfaced lane to the left of the beck across from the New Inn eliminates some road walking, rejoining the tarmac lane at a footbridge after about 400 metres. Cross the busy Clapham by-pass where traffic travels at high speed (the A65) with care; cognoscenti use the safer cattle underpass by the stream reached by a gate to the left.

You'll have checked your train times carefully. If they are not convenient (in recent years the Lancaster line has seen cuts in service) Pennine Buses also go to Settle and Skipton from the bus stop near the post office every two hours to link with trains (less frequent on Sundays).

29. DENT

As much an excuse to enjoy a trip on the spectacular Settle-Carlisle line as to enjoy a pint of Dent Bitter in one of the loveliest of the Yorkshire Dales.

Pub: The Sportsman's Inn, Cowgill, Dent. Dent Brewery Bitter; Younger's Scotch bitter; Younger's No 3; Open Monday to Saturday 1100 – 1500 (closed Monday lunchtime) and 1900 – 2300; Sunday 1200 – 1500 and 1900 – 2230. Food daily 1200 – 1400 and 1900-2100.

Start: Dent Station.

Distance: $4^1/_2$ miles (7 km)

Maps: Outdoor Leisure: Sheet 2 Yorkshire Dales Western Area. Landranger: Sheet 98

Public Transport: Dent Station is on the Leeds-Settle-Carlisle Line (BR Table 36) through service from Manchester/Blackpool on certain summer Saturdays

By Car: To drive to Dent is to miss much of the point of the trip; however, for the sacrilegious, parking can be found close to Dent Station (Dent Station car park is for rail users only).

Whether you come north from Leeds or Settle or south from Carlisle, a trip on the legendary Settle and Carlisle Railway is an experience to tempt more than rail buffs, being one of the most exhilarating train journeys in England. This short walk can easily be timed to enjoy a glimpse of what Dentdale has to offer and a pint of Dent bitter to boot, and either return or continue your trip onto Carlisle or Settle to enjoy the whole line.

Highest Railway station

Alight at Dent Station, England's highest railway station at 1,145 feet above sea level and over four miles from the village it serves. The views

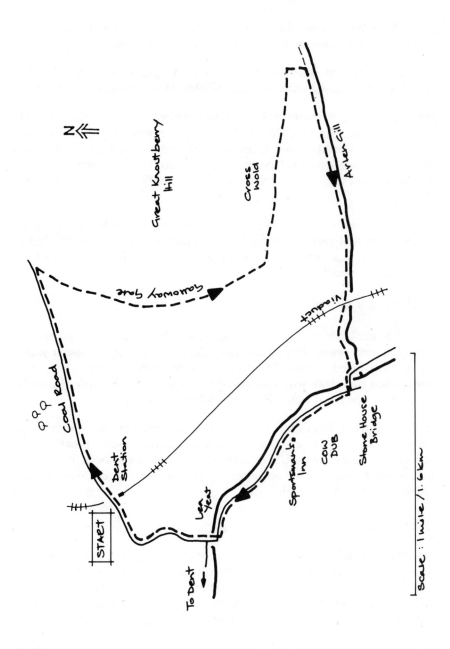

from the station down the long green curve of Dentdale, between the mountains to the distant Howgills, are truly memorable.

Notice the Station Master's house on the right, supposedly the first house in England with double glazing when it was built in the 1870s.

From the Station exit turn right, and make your way uphill along what is still known as The Coal Road. This was the former packhorse track which linked Dentdale and Garsdale with the old coal pits on Cowgill Wold, and once provided communities in both valleys with coal. It's now asphalted and carries local and tourist traffic despite murderously steep gradients.

Follow the road uphill for about three quarters of a mile, (which given the gradient will seem very much longer) past a plantation on the left to a junction with a broad green track on the right, usually churned up with vehicular tracks.

Galloway Gate

Take this track, right, which soon becomes a broad green way between widely spaced walls. This is Galloway Gate, so named because it was a drove road, used in the 18th century by Scottish drovers. They came down from Galloway with vast herds of cattle for the English Midlands, heading for the great Cattle Fairs on Malham Moor.

Follow the track through a gate and as it contours around the hillside, the track now open to your right, and offering quite breathtaking, panoramic views across Upper Dentdale. The green bulk of Whernside and other peaks rise in sequence along Dentdale and down to the rounded summits of the Howgills.

Arten Gill

The track virtually follows the 1,700 foot contour round the shoulder of Great Knoutberry Hill, going through another gate to re-enter an enclosed track, and bearing eastwards as it descends Cross Wold, now sloping down into the valley of Arten Gill, finally turning sharply right and meeting the stony track along Arten Gill itself.

Turn right here. Gallowaygate once continued directly ahead but its route is now obscured. Your way is along another ancient, stony way this time the road which once linked Dent with the town of Hawes via Widdale, and which remains a superb walk between Dentdale and Wensleydale.

Viaduct

The track becomes a steep and stony way and heads through a gate before descending to the magnificently proportioned Arten Gill Viaduct on the Settle Carlisle line, one of the finest of the line's architectural features. Its 11 arches are 117 feet high at their highest point. It is built of largely of Dent Marble, a locally quarried limestone which is dark grey or black in colour because of carbon impurities. It was once highly prized as a decorative stone, being polished for use for in ornamental fireplaces and table tops.

You may be lucky enough to see a train pass over the viaduct. Sadly modern Sprinter diesel rail-cars, though fast and efficient, have none of the glamour of steam nor even of the recently retired big diesel locomotives, which replaced steam on the S&C engines in the 1960s and until 1990.

As you go under the arches note a tiny beck, Arten Gill. In the early part of last century there was a small mill here whose ruins can just be traced, originally with an iron water wheel used to power spinning jennies. In 1835 a young Tyneside engineer, William George Armstrong, came on a fishing and walking holiday here with his young wife and spent time studying the wheel and calculated it was using only one twentieth of its available power. This led him to consider more efficient ways of harnessing water power, and led directly to the invention of a rotary hydraulic machine, the precursor of the modern turbine. Armstrong went on to become one of the greatest engineers of his day and founder of the great engineering company that bore his name, and it all began in Arten Gill in Dentdale.

You reach the valley bottom at Stone House Bridge. Turn right in the lane and follow it alongside the little River Dee. This section of the walk follows the Dales Way. After about five minutes walk you reach Cow Dub and the traditional white walled farmhouse style tavern, the

Sportsman's Inn, a listed 18th century building in a superb position. It is sometimes known by locals as "The Dub", a name which comes from Celtic and refers to a nearby pool in the river.

There's excellent ale and good food on offer and if you find you can't face the walk back up to Dent station, there is overnight accommodation available.

Otherwise give yourself plenty of time (at least 45 minutes) before your train. Go left outside the pub along the lane for just under half a mile to Lea Yeat, where you turn right up the Coal Road on the Garsdale Road to Dent Station, a very steep climb as the lane twists uphill at a gradient of 1 in 4 and perhaps worse on the bends. When you finally have given up hope of getting to the top, the rooftop of Dent station comes into view and if you've allowed sufficient time to catch your breath you might even enjoy those views again before the return train. Volunteers have restored the waiting room on the Settle-bound platform, particularly welcome on wet days, and there's even a little information point inside to encourage a return visit to Dent.

Steam on the Settle-Carlisle Railway - an historic shot.

30. DUFTON

A walk from Appleby Station on the Settle-Carlisle line to the edge of the North Pennines through the lovely red sandstone country of the Eden Valley.

Pub: The Midland, Appleby Station. Marstons Pedigree, Marston's Best Bitter, Marstons Mild. Open Monday to Saturday 1145 – 2300; Sunday 1200 – 1500 and 1900 – 2230.

Food daily when the pub is open.

Start: Appleby Station

Distance: 8 miles (13 km)

Maps: OS Landranger Sheet 91 Appleby; Pathfinder Sheet 587

Public Transport: Settle-Carlisle Line to Appleby (BR Table 36)

By Car: Park in Appleby Station Yard

All that was said about the Settle-Carlisle in Walk 29 applies to this Walk 30. The trip to Appleby will allow you to travel even more of this remarkable railway line, including the impressive Mallerstang valley.

The Midland Hotel at Appleby, a typical railway pub built with comfortable Cumbrian red sandstone, lies just beyond the station. With its pleasant beer garden around the back of the pub, a choice of very good food and drink (coffee is available and excellent Marston's ales which must surely originally have come from Burton, which also lies on the Midland Railway) a visit is as tempting at the start as at the end of a walk. Some people may even consider doing both.

The walk itself, with its spectacular views of the North Pennines, is a particular favourite, and is a fitting way to and any book about Pub Walks in the Pennines. It is timed to fit in with trains, but pathfinding

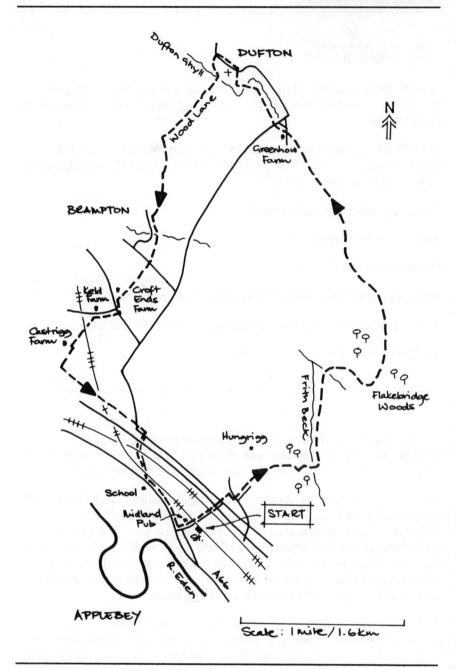

needs care and large scale maps are recommended, even though some waymarking is in evidence.

From Appleby Station cross the footbridge if you arrive from the Settle direction (or are leaving the Midland Hotel), to take the rear entrance from the southbound platform onto a lane, turning right and soon passing the old Appleby East (Warcop branch) station. As the road bends, take the path ahead signed for Hunrigg which crosses the busy Appleby by-pass (A66). Cross with great care, following stiles to the next lane ahead which is also crossed, keeping ahead to a second lane where you turn right. Follow this almost to a junction where an enclosed path, left, leads down to another stile.

Frith Beck

The path, marked by white waymarks, goes straight ahead across a field, with the first of several superb panoramic views ahead of the North Pennine escarpments that dominate this walk. The great domelike hills in the foreground are Dufton and Murton Pikes. The path swings right at the top of the field to enter a wood at a gate and stile. Descend the edge of this pretty wood to a stile below, and cross the field ahead and half hidden bridge over a stream, Frith Beck. Turn left alongside the stream, eventually joining a track running alongside a wood. Keep ahead through a gate, the track curving across another stream to a junction of tracks. Turn right along the forest track into Flakebridge Woods. This beautiful wood is currently being felled and replanted, but keeps much of its charm.

You soon pass an old mill, now a farm, but at the second farmhouse take the track left, uphill, through extensively cleared areas. After about 350 metres, the path bears off right just to the right of a small pond, not easy to find, make for the second of two gates in the wall on the right. Keep ahead to a stile in the wall ahead, and follows the edge of the wood until a stile on the left leads down to a shallow ravine and stream crossed by a footbridge. Contour round right and now follow the wall along the bottom of a long field. The path and wall gradually curves to the left; ignore a tempting gate to the right but take the next one leading into a field of tree stumps. From here it is fairly straightforward through a succession of stiles and through gates to Greenhow Farm ahead. Immediately past the farm, a gap stile leads to a narrow path by a stream that crosses the lane ahead. Go through stiles into Dufton Ghyll, a secret, red sandstone ravine, thickly wooded, which is massed with bluebells in Spring.

Keep ahead along the path between sandstone cliffs to a footbridge at the bottom of the Ghyll where you should cross and follow the track uphill until it bears right into Dufton village. This is a former lead miners' village built around extensive green. It has a particular charm with its red sandstone cottages and handsome fountain, village pub. The farmhouse at the top left hand corner of the village (looking northwards) sells tea and scones to ramblers during the summer and there is a village shop.

The route back to Appleby begins by this farmhouse, along the signed track which drops back down into the Ghyll to another bridge. Climb directly ahead, past a crossing of tracks and along a beautiful green road, Wood Lane. Follow it as it curves left towards Brampton. Where you eventually meet a sharp T-junction turn left down to a ford with a footbridge 50 metres to the left. Cross here and bear right, but look for a stile in the wall left leading to fieldpath up to the lane west of Brampton. A few metres to the left is another field path, signed, which bears right to a stile and then keeps ahead up a long field to Croft End farm ahead.

Castrigg Farm

Turn left into the road for 100 metres, but take the first track right past Keld Farm, soon after which a stile, waymarked, leads to a path across to the railway. Cross, over the next stile left, turning right with waymarks up the hedge past Castrigg Farm to the next stile. Keep ahead to descend another long field where a hurdle stile is on the right just before the field corner, and cross another stile left into a broad track, running between deep hedges. This is High Street, part of the Roman Road between Brough and Carlisle.

Turn left along this lovely old way by deep hedgerows, back over the railway line until you emerge on the outskirts of Appleby. Turn right at the junction and follow the road under the new bypass and railway into the edge of the town, joining the old A66 road below Appleby Grammar School.

At the bottom of the hill a footway on the left marked by finer posts leads to steps by a small garden and into Clifford Street to the Midland Hotel and that pint of Pedigree (and the station) but if you've got time available, use it to explore the old town of Appleby as well, reached by turning right over the river bridge ahead.

Appleby

Appleby-in-Westmorland is a fine old town, rich in heritage interest, with a lovely old marketplace, old shops, (one of them medieval) a magnificent medieval church, unusual 17th century almshouses, and a castle with a Tower like the Tower of London which goes back to Norman times (the grounds are now a rare breeds park), and riverside and woodland walks. Just keep an eye on the clock to make sure you get your train, as it's a good ten minutes' uphill walk from the marketplace.

The Rambler Inn, Edale: a popular stopping-off point on the Pennine Way

Other Sigma Leisure titles...

Why not try some of the other books in this selection from the range of popular *Sigma Leisure* titles?

West Cheshire Walks	*Jen Darling*
East Cheshire Walks	*Graham Beech*
West Pennine Walks	*Mike Cresswell*
Newark & Sherwood Rambles	*Malcolm McKenzie*
Pub Walks in Cheshire	*Jen Darling*
Pub Walks in Lancashire	*Neil Coates*
Pub Walks in the Peak District	*Les Lumsdon & Martin Smith*
Pub Walks in the Pennines	*Les Lumsdon & Colin Speakman*
Rambles Around Manchester	*Mike Cresswell*
Herefordshire Walks	*Les Lumsdon*
Western Lakeland Rambles	*Gordon Brown*
Off-Beat Cycling and Mountain Biking in the Peak National Park	*Clive Smith*

All available from good booksellers, but in case of difficulty, why not write to us or telephone us? - We will be happy to help!

24hr. inquiry/order service. Access/Visa welcome.
Complete Catalogue on request.

Sigma Leisure, 1 South Oak Lane, Wilmslow, Cheshire, SK9 6AR.
Tel: *(0625) 531035*, Fax: (0625) 536800.

An Invitation

Sigma Leisure is expanding and always on the lookout for new books, and of course, new authors to write them!

Our current range includes:

- ❏ An extensive range of rambling books

- ❏ Our very popular range of "Pub Walks"

- ❏ Town & Village guides to the North West

- ❏ Books on local interest and history

- ❏ Activity interests such as Mountain Biking

Future publications include:

- ❏ Great Moments for Manchester United, and Manchester City

- ❏ Myths and Legends of East Cheshire and the Moorlands

Our speed of production and successful marketing could make a great success of your book. So if you are interested, and have an idea for a book for the leisure market, then why not telephone us on *(0625) 531035* for further information or alternatively, write to us at our office:

Sigma Leisure,
1 South Oak Lane, Wilmslow, Cheshire, SK9 6AR
Fax: (0625) 536800

CUSTOMER QUESTIONNAIRE

Please take a few moments to complete this questionnaire – you'll help us a lot, and you might win yourself a bottle of bubbly!

1 a Is this your first purchase of a Sigma Leisure book? YES☐ NO☐

b If no, how many Sigma Leisure books have you purchased before? ☐

2 Please indicate your **main** reason for purchasing this book:

a	for use with an Ordnance Survey map	☐
b	as an alternative to a map for use on walks	☐
c	for reference to local features of interest only	☐
d	as a souvenir of a holiday	☐
e	as a gift	☐
f	other, please specify	

3 Tick **three** main reasons why you selected this particular book:

a	price	☐
b	cover design	☐
c	presentation	☐
d	content	☐
e	recommended by a friend	☐
f	assistance given in the shop	☐
g	author	☐
h	quality of information	☐
i	illustrations	☐
j	other, please specify	

4 Do you think this book is:

a	good value for money	☐
b	fair value for money	☐
c	poor value for money	☐

Continued overleaf . . .

5 Which features of the book do you like most? Please list in order of priority, i.e. 1 to 8, 1 being the highest priority.

a   binding
b   layout
c   illustrations/photographs
d   cover design
e   size
f   detail of information
g   easy to follow
h   content
i   other, please specify

6 Do you think the book can be improved in any of the following areas:

a   binding
b   layout
c   cover design
d   illustrations/photographs
e   size
f   detail of information
g   ease of use
h   content
i   other, please specify

Any further comments:

Please return this questionnaire to: Sigma Press, 1 South Oak Lane, Wilmslow, Cheshire SK9 6AR. If you would like a copy of our catalogue plus the chance to win a bottle of champagne, please fill in your name and address, below. The first three names drawn out of the hat on 1st December 1991 win the bubbly!

Name:
Address: